MACROECONOMICS

Arjun Y. Pangannavar

ATLANTIC
PUBLISHERS & DISTRIBUTORS (P) LTD

Published by
ATLANTIC
PUBLISHERS & DISTRIBUTORS (P) LTD
7/22, Ansari Road, Darya Ganj,
New Delhi-110002
Phones : +91-11-40775252, 23273880, 23275880, 23280451
Fax : +91-11-23285873
Web : www.atlanticbooks.com
E-mail : orders@atlanticbooks.com

Branch Office
5, Nallathambi Street, Wallajah Road,
Chennai-600002
Phones : +91-44-64611085, 32413319
E-mail : chennai@atlanticbooks.com

Printed in India at Glorious Printers, A-13, D.S.I.D.C., Jhilmil Industrial Area, Delhi-11009

Dedicated to

My father
Late Shri Yallappa Ningappa Pangannavar
and
Mother Late Smt. Holhevva

Preface

It gives me immense pleasure to bring out this book on macroeconomics to fufil the needs of students of economics pursuing graduation under semester system. It is designed as per the syllabi of Karnatak University, Dharwad and Rani Chennamma University, Belgaum prescribed for BA Fifth Semester economics course. It is hoped that the book will also be helpful to the students studying economics in other universities in Arts and Commerce faculties. Besides, it will be useful to those who are preparing for competitive examinations.

The book consists of five chapters. First chapter covers the meaning, definitions, subject matter and scope of macroeconomics and national income studies. Second chapter presents a detailed discussion on classical theory of income and employment. Third chapter deals with Keynesian economics, including income and employment theory, consumption function, investment function and investment multiplier theory. Fourth chapter throws light on acceleration principle, k and v interaction and savings and investment controversy. Fifth chapter explains in detail, the trade cycles and the theories on trade cycle. A new approach is used to make this book more comprehensible and making the learning of economics easy. It is a student-friendly and teacher-friendly book.

I am grateful to able teachers and other experts on the subject who extended their helpful suggestions during the writing of this book, enriching its contents. I am also thankful to Atlantic Publishers and Distributors (P) Ltd. for the interest evinced in publishing the book. Suggestions for further improvement of the book in subsequent editions are welcome.

Arjun Y. Pangannavar

Contents

1

Macroeconomics and National Income

1.1 MACROECONOMICS

Modern economic analysis has been classified broadly into two categories, viz. (i) Microeconomics and (ii) Macroeconomics. These terms were first used by Prof. Ragner Frisch of Oslo University in 1933. He used the terms to explain the modern approach to the study of economics. Microeconomic approach is a traditional approach to the study of economics. It has been developed by economists like Ricardo, Marshall, and Pigou. Macroeconomic approach is a modern approach to the study of economics. It is a recent development. It became popular after the publication of the book *General Theory of Employment, Interest and Money* by J.M. Keynes in 1936.

1.1.1 Meaning of Macroeconomics

The term "Macro" has been derived from a Greek word "MAKROS" that means "Large". Macroeconomics may be described as that branch of economic analysis which studies the economic behaviour not of the individual small units or components of the economy but of the economic system as a whole. In other words, macroeconomics is a study of aggregates like Total Consumption, Total Production, Total Savings, Total Investments, Total Employment, Total Income, etc.

J.M. Keynes, the 20th century economist, has popularized macroeconomics through his economic theories after the publication of his famous book *General Theory of Employment Interest and Money* in 1936.

1.1.2 Definitions of Macroeconomics

The following are the main definitions of macroeconomics:

(i) **Prof. Boulding** defined macroeconomics as "Macroeconomics does not deal with the individual quantities as such but with the aggregates of these quantities, not with individual income but with national income, not with individual prices but with general price level, not with individual output but with the national output".

(ii) **Prof. Mac-Connell** defines it as "In dealing with the aggregates, Macroeconomics is concerned with obtaining an overview or general outline of the structure of the economy and the relationship between the major aggregates, in short. It examines the forest as whole and not individual trees. It gives bird's eye view of the economy."

(iii) **Prof. Ackley Gardner** defined it as "Macroeconomics deals with economic affairs in the large".

In brief, it concerns with the aggregates of economic values. It looks at the total size and shape of the entire but not its individual parts. It studies the character of the entire forest but not its individual trees.

1.1.3 Scope of Macroeconomics

The scope of macroeconomics means the field of study of macroeconomics. It covers the following:

(i) Theory of Income, Output and Employment which also covers (a) Theory of Consumption Function, (b) Theory of Investment Function, and (c) Theory of Trade Cycles.

(ii) Theory of Prices that consists of (a) Theories of Inflation (b) Theories of Deflation, and (c) Theories of Reflation.

(iii) Theory of Economic Growth that is applicable to developed and underdeveloped countries.

(iv) Theory of Distribution which relates to (a) share of wages in total national income, and (b) share of profits in total national income.

Since macroeconomics is mainly concerned with income and employment, it is also known as the theory of income and employment.

1.1.4 Types of Macroeconomics

There are three types of macroeconomics. These are as follows:

(i) **Macro Static:** It is used to explain the aggregative relations in a stationary state. It deals with the final equilibrium of the economy at a particular point of time.

(ii) **Comparative Macro Static:** It involves a comparative study of different equilibriums attained by the economy.

(iii) **Macro Dynamics:** It relates to the changes in macro variables and aggregates.

1.1.5 Uses or Importance of Macroeconomics

The following are the uses or importance of macroeconomics:

(i) **It Gives Complete Picture:** Macroeconomics helps us to get a clear and complete picture of the economy as a whole. It is useful to understand the functioning of the economy, because it deals with the aggregative variables.

(ii) **It is Useful for Formulating of Economic Policies:** Macroeconomics is useful to the formulation of economic policies of a country. For example, monetary policy, employment policy, trade policies, etc.

(iii) **It Helps to Study the 'Economic Growth':** It studies the economic growth. By studying national income and generation of employment, government formulates the proper policies for economic growth.

(iv) **It Helps to Give Solutions of Economic Problems:** Macroeconomics deals with several economic problems of the economy. It also provides proper solutions to them.

(v) **It is Useful to Study Trade Cycles:** Macroeconomics studies the fluctuations in broad economic aggregates. It also considers the causes and effects of the trade cycles.

(vi) **It Helps to Study the Effects of Inflation and Deflation:** Macroeconomics help us to understand the effects of inflation and deflation. It also assists to undertake measures to control them.

(vii) **Helps Microeconomic Analysis:** Macroeconomic analysis helps the development of microeconomics. For example, the law of diminishing marginal utility could not have been formulated without studying the behaviour of masses of individuals.

1.1.6 Limitations or Criticisms of Macroeconomics

Macroeconomics suffers certain limitations so it has been criticized as under:

(i) **It Suffers from Excessive Generalization:** Macroeconomics suffers from danger of excessive generalizations. What is true of a whole economy may not be true of an individual. For example, what is true of the entire forest may not be true of a tree. From the study of aggregates, general conclusions cannot be made about the individual unit.

(ii) **It Derives Wrong Conclusions:** The study of aggregates some-times leads us to wrong conclusions. For example, if agricultural prices have fallen by 50 per cent and industrial prices have risen by 50 per cent, the general price level would remain unchanged. From this we may come to the conclusion that no section of the community has been affected. But our conclusion would be wrong because the agriculturists have lost their income and industrialists have gained. Therefore, aggregative results would mislead us.

(iii) **It Neglects the Structure of Aggregates:** The structure of aggregates is more important than the aggregate itself. For example, there may be a rise in the general price level. But it does not mean that all the sectors of the economy have been benefited equally. Under such cases, it is necessary to break the aggregates into its component parts.

(iv) **It is Associated with the Problem of Aggregation:** The Macroeconomics deals with aggregates. For example, aggregate consumption, savings and investments but all these factors consist of heterogeneous elements so they create problem of exact conclusion. For example, one cannot draw conclusion on the basis of aggregate consumption because the consumer behaviour differs from person to person.

(v) **Macroeconomic Models are Useful Only to Developed Countries:** The macroeconomic models are more useful in advanced countries when compared with under developed countries. For example, Keynes' investment multiplier theory cannot work in poor countries because the marginal propensity to consume is greater than one.

1.2 NATIONAL INCOME

1.2.1 Meaning and Definitions

Meaning. The concept of National Income occupies an important place in economic theory. National income means the total income of the people of the nation in a year. In real terms, national income is the flow of goods and services produced in an economy in a particular year.

More elaborately, national income is a money measure of value of net aggregate of goods and services becoming available annually to the nation as a result of the economic activities of the community at large, consisting of households or individuals, business firms and social and political institutions.

National income is variously described, sometimes it is known as "national income" at other times, "national product" or "national dividend". As a matter of fact, all these terms mean one and the same thing.

Definitions

There are various definitions of national income which can be grouped into two categories: (i) traditional definitions, and (ii) modern definitions.

(i) *Traditional Definitions*

The following are the important traditional definitions of national income:

(a) Alfred Marshall's Definition

Alfred Marshall defines national income as "The labour and capital of a country acting on its natural resources produce annually a certain net aggregate of commodities, material and immaterial including services of all kinds.... This is the true net annual income or revenue of the country or national dividend."

In this definition, the word 'net' refers to deductions from the gross national income in respect of depreciation and wearing out of machines. And to this must be added income from abroad.

No doubt, Marshall's definition is theoretically sound, simple and comprehensive; even then it has serious practical limitations. (i) It is not easy to make substantially correct estimate of total production of goods and services in a country, (ii) there are some commodities substantial part of which does not become available for sale in the market and, (iii) the danger of double counting.

(b) A.C. Pigou's Definition

A.C. Pigou defines national income as "National income is that part of objective income of the community, including of course income derived from abroad which can be measured in money". This definition is better than Marshallian definition. It is more practical also. Pigou's definition took into account (i) income received on account of investment in foreign countries and (ii) only that income of country which can be measured in terms of money are to be included in national income while estimating it.

Though Pigou's definition is precise, convenient, elastic, and workable, it suffers from certain drawbacks: (i) it is applicable to developed countries but not to the backward underdeveloped countries where the barter system exists, and (ii) it is applicable to such commodities that can be exchanged for money. According to Pigou, a woman's services as a nurse would be included in national income when worked for money but it cannot be included when she worked it for her child at home. Thus, the Pigovian definition gives rise to a good number of paradoxes.

(c) Irving Fisher's Definition

Irving Fisher defines national income as "The national dividend or income consists solely of services as received by ultimate consumers, whether from their material or from their human environments." Thus, a piano or an over coat made for me this year is not a part of this year's income, but an addition to capital. Only the services rendered to me during this year by the things are income: According to Fisher, the national income of a country is determined not by its annual production but by its annual consumptions. For example, the value of piano manufactured in 1975 is ₹ 2000. According to Marshall, the entire ₹ 2000 would be taken in the national income of 1975. But according to Fisher, only the actual money value of consumption of piano in 1975 would be included in the national income of that year. Suppose the life of the piano is 20 years, then the money value of consumption of the piano in 1975 would be ₹ 100. So, with the production of piano the national income for 1975 would increase by only ₹ 100 and not by ₹ 2000. Though Fisher's approach is better and scientific and reasonable in practical life, it will be very difficult to calculate the money value of the consumption of goods and services.

No one definition discussed above is comprehensive but each definition has element of truth. The choice of a definition is just a matter of the purpose pursued by the economist. In brief, Marshall and Pigou have defined national income in terms of production but Fisher has defined it in terms of the consumption of goods and services.

(ii) *Modern Definitions*

Modern economist Simon Kuznets has defined national income as "the net output of commodities and services flowing during the year from the country's productive system in the hands of consumers".

Modern economy is money economy. Thus, national income of the country is expressed in money terms. A National Sample Survey has defined national income as "Money measures of the net aggregates of all commodities and services accruing to the inhabitants of a community during a specified period".

1.2.2 Elements of National Income

The discussion on above definitions of national income brings out three points:

(i) National income refers to the income of the country.

(ii) Its measurement refers to a specific period of time, say, a year.

(iii) National income includes all types of goods and services which have an exchange value, counting each one of them only once.

(iv) Only those incomes connected with all economic activities are included in national income.

(v) The capital gains made by an individual have also to be excluded from the national income of the country because such capital gains do not represent any productive capacity on the part of individual concerned.

(vi) The income accruing to an individual from illegal activities such as black marketing and smuggling has also to be excluded because such an income does not result from socially useful economic activities.

(vii) No commodities or services should be counted twice or more, otherwise the result will not be accurate. For example, if raw cotton has been evaluated in agricultural production, it should not be included while calculating total value of the cotton textiles.

Generally, two statistical methods are used to avoid double counting or multiple counting in the calculation of national income (i) final products methods, and (ii) value, added method.

According to the value-added method, we add up the value of final products only. Final products are those which are finally consumed by the consumer.

According to the value-added method, we do not take into account the value of the final goods and services produced in the country. On the contrary, we go on adding the value created at each stage in the manufacture of a commodity. Then all such values accruing in all processes in the manufacture of all commodities are added up together to arrive at the national income of the country.

1.2.3 Concepts of National Income

The following are the various concepts of national income.

(a) *Gross National Product (GNP)*

The Gross National Product is the basic social accounting measure. It is the nation's total production of goods and services produced in a year assessed in terms of the market prices. It includes all the economic productions in the economy during one year. In other words, the GNP is the money value of the total national production of goods and services produced in a given period.

While calculating GNP, we must take into account that:

(i) Money value of the final goods and services should only be taken into account to avoid double counting or multiple counting. Final goods and services are those which are finally consumed by the consumers. No intermediate goods and services are taken into account. For example, bread is a final good but flour is an intermediate good.

(ii) We must take into account the money value of only currently produced goods and service while estimating GNP.

(iii) The use of the word 'Gross' should be particularly noted in relation to the term GNP. This means in computing the GNP we do not deduct the depreciation or replacement of fixed assets.

Thus, GNP = NNP + DC

where GNP = Gross National Product

NNP = Net National Product

DC = Depreciation Costs

GNP can also be computed as:

$$GNP = C + I + G + (X - M) + (R - P)$$

where, C = Consumption Goods

I = Investment or Capital Goods

G = Government Services
X = Exports
M = Imports
R = Receipts from Foreign Countries
P = Payments made to Foreign Countries

When the net income earned from foreign countries (R – P) is deducted from GNP and the net government subsidies is added to it, we get Gross Domestic Product (GDP), i.e. GDP = C + I + G + (R – P) + (S – IDT), where S = Subsidies, IDT = Indirect taxes.

(b) *Net National Product (NNP)*

Net national product is the net production of goods and services in a country during the year. It is GNP minus the value of capital consumed or depreciated during the year. So it can be calculated as:

$$NNP = GNP - DC$$

NNP is also called national income at market prices. NNP is better concept than GNP, because it makes proper allowances for the depreciation suffered by machinery, equipment, building etc., during the year. The concept is highly useful as it gives an idea of net increase in the total production of the country. It also proves helpful in the analysis of the long-run problem of maintaining and increasing the supply of physical capital in the country. NNP is highly useful concept in the study of 'Growth Economics'. But this concept of NNP has the complex problem of fixing appropriate rates of depreciation of plants, equipment, building, etc. in the economy.

(c) *National Income (NI) or National Income at Factor Cost*

It is also known as national income at factor cost. National income is the total of all income payments received by the factors of production, viz. land, labour, capital and organization. It can be derived from the NNP in the following manner.

National Income = NNP – Indirect Taxes + Subsidies – Profits Accruing to the Government.

$$NI = NNP - IDT + SDs - PG$$

As we have seen already, GNP is arrived at by computing the end products without depreciating and NNP is arrived by subtracting depreciation. But the whole of NNP is not available for distribution among the four factors of production. The firms have to pay indirect taxes (on their goods and services) to the government. This sum does not go to the factors of production. These indirect taxes have to be deducted from the NNP to find out the national income. Sometimes the government also gives subsidies on the production of certain goods and services. In other words, the production cost of the goods and services are higher, but on account of governmental subsidies they are sold in the market at prices lower than their actual production costs. Though these goods and services are sold at lower prices, yet the factors producing them are paid higher rewards on account of subsidies paid by the government under these circumstances if we wish to find out the income of the various factors, we will have to add the amount of government subsidies to the market value of the NNP.

The government runs various types of industries, business enterprises and transport, etc. The profit earned by the government from these enterprises does not go to the factors of production. They accrue to the government. As such they should be deducted from the NNP to arrive at national income at factor cost.

The concept of national income throws light on the distribution side of the national income. It tells us how the national output is distribution among the various factors of production in lieu of the services rendered by them. As such it is closely related with the concept of economic justice.

(d) *Personal Income (PI)*

Personal income is the national income which is actually received by the individuals or households after certain deductions made from it. Whole of the national income earned by the factors of production in one year is not available to them. Several deductions are made out of it. For example, corporate income taxes have to be paid out of corporation profit before they are distributed among the shareholders. Likewise, a part of the corporate profit may be retained undistributed by the corporation. Similarly, the workers and salaried employees have to make certain social security contributions such as provident or pension funds. To the extent of these deductions, the income is not available to the community. The government may also give some social security benefits such as unemployment allowances, old age pensions, etc. These payments are called transfer payments. These are to be added to arrive at personal income. The following formula is used to calculate PI.

Personal Income = National Income – Corporate Income Taxes – Undistributed Corporate Profits – Social Security Contributions + Transfer Payments.

$$PI = NI - CIT - UDCP - SSCs + TPs$$

The concept of personal income is useful in estimating the potential purchasing power of the households in an economy. The weakness of this concept is that it does not clearly tell us the actual amount of money available to the households for spending and saving. To know that we shall have to find out disposable income of the household.

(e) *Disposable Personal Income (DPI)*

The entire personal income is not available for consumption to the individuals because part of it has to be paid to the government by way of personal direct taxes. The actual amount that is available to the individuals for use after payment of personal direct taxes is called 'Disposable Personal Incomes'. In other words, it is the actual amount available to the individuals or community for use after paying personal direct taxes.

Therefore, Disposable Personal Income = Personal Income – Personal Direct Taxes.

$$DPI = PI - DT$$

But it is not essential that the whole of the disposable personal income is spent on consumption alone. Generally, individuals spend a major portion of DPI on consumption, reserving the remainder for saving. Thus, it can also be written as:

$$DPI = Y = C + S$$

where C = Consumption, S = Savings

1.2.4 Methods of Estimating National Income

The concept of the national income involves three interpretations: (i) It represents the monetary value of aggregate annual production in the country. (ii) It represents aggregate income of the country. (iii) It represents the aggregate expenditure in the economy. Whatever may be the interpretation the result is the same because every expenditure at the same time is receipts and then both expenditures and receipts are equivalent to the value of goods and services exchanged between the buyers and the sellers. This threefold interpretation of national income has, thus, given rise to three methods of measuring it. They are: (i) Census of Production Method, (ii) Census of Income Method and (iii) Census of Expenditure Method.

(i) *Census of Production Method or Output Method*

This method measures the output of the country. It is also called the inventory method. Under this method, national income can be estimated through census of the gross value of production of goods and services produced in different economic sector by all productive enterprises in the economy. For example, the income from the sectors like agriculture, forestry, fisheries, mining, industries, transport, commerce and other services are computed added to estimate the national income.

To the aggregated value of total output, net income earned from abroad, i.e. net difference between the value of exports and imports is added. Indirect taxes like excise and custom duties and depreciation charges are to be deducted from the total income estimated. Thus, the national income estimation under product method is shown as follow:

$$Y = (P - D) + (S - T) + [(X - M) + (R - P)]$$

where

Y = Total Income of the Nation,

P = Domestic Output of All Production Sectors

D = Depreciation Charges

S = Subsidies

T = Indirect Taxes

X = Exports

M = Imports
R = Receipts from Abroad, and
P = Payments made to Abroad

But under this method there is certain danger of double counting. So the following precautions are necessary:

(i) To avoid double counting, we must add only the final products. Raw materials and intermediate goods should not be included.

(ii) Goods for self-consumption by the producer should be excluded; they have not been marketed, so it is difficult to ascertain their true market value.

(iii) While evaluating the output changes in the price levels between the years must be taken into account. It is usual to denote the national income with reference to a particular year.

(iv) The indirect taxes included in prices are to be deducted for getting exact market value of the products. Similarly, subsidies given by the government to certain products should be added in evaluating the product.

(v) Add the value of export, or the income earned abroad, deduct the value of imports.

This method is widely used in the underdeveloped countries, but it is less reliable because the margin of error in this method is large. However, this method is applied to estimate the income from agriculture, mining and manufacturing, including handicrafts.

Generally, two statistical methods are used to avoid double counting in the calculation of national income: (a) Final product method, and (b) Value-added method.

Under the final product method, the value of only final products are add up. We first take the total value of final consumer goods produced in the country during the year. Then, we add the total value of durable producer goods such as machinery and plants, etc. to it. This will give us aggregate value of all final goods produced in the country during the year.

Under value-added method, we do not take into account the value of the final goods and services produced in the country. Instead of it, we go on adding the values created at each stage in the manufacture of a commodity. It is illustrated in the following example:

Let us suppose that a ready-made cotton shirt passes through four stages of production. In the first stage, the farmer produces raw cotton from the soil. In the second stage, the cotton is converted into cotton cloth in a factory. In the third stage, the cotton cloth is converted into a bush-shirt by the ready-made garments firm. In the fourth stage, the ready-made bush-shirt is sold to a retailer from whom it is finally purchased by the customer. Now only the money value added in the various stages of production of cotton shirt should be added up while making the estimate of the national income of the country. This can be illustrated with the help of Table 1.1.

Table 1.1: Value-Added Method

Sl. No.	Stages of production	Sale value of the cotton shirt (in ₹)	Increase in value (in ₹)
1.	Cotton growing farmer	5	5
2.	Cloth manufacturing factory	10	5
3.	Ready-made garment firm	15	5
4.	Retailer	20	5
	Total	50	20

If we add values at all stages of production of the cotton shirt, the aggregate comes to ₹ 50. But when we take into account of the value-added at each stage of production the total values added is ₹ 20 for the cotton shirt. Whether we adopt the final or the value-added method, the result will be the same.

(ii) *Census of Income Method*

Under this method, national income is computed from the side of incomes, i.e. from the side of distribution of income. According to this method, the national income is calculated by adding up the incomes of all individuals in the country as productive agents. Individuals earn an income either by contributing their own services or by providing the services of their property such as land and capital in the production.

Therefore, national income is calculated by adding up the incomes of all individuals in the form of rent wages and salaries, interest and profit.

National income under this method is calculated by adding up the following different types of incomes:

(i) Rent of land.

(ii) Wages and salaries of persons employed. Pensions are excluded as they represent mere transfer payments.

(iii) Interest on capital.

(iv) Profit of entrepreneurs including undistributed profits of joint stock companies and earning of self-employed people like doctors, lawyers, dramatists, cultivators, etc.

(v) Incomes from overseas investments.

The following formula is used to calculate the national income:

$$Y = \sum (w+r+i+\eta) + [(X-M) + (R-P)]$$

where

w = wages, r = rent, i = interest, η = profits

However, certain precautions are necessary while following this method.

(i) All transfer payments (government and personal) like gift, pension, etc. are to be deducted. Similarly, gambling, being transfer activity is to be excluded.

(ii) All unpaid services (like services of housewife) are to be excluded. Only those services for which payments are made should be included.

(iii) Financial transactions and sales of old property (including land) are to be excluded, as they do not add anything to the national income. Thus, all capital gains and losses which are related to wealth but not real income should be excluded.

(iv) Direct tax revenue to the government should be subtracted from the total income as it is only a transfer of income.

(v) Similarly, government subsidies should be deducted.

(vi) Add the value of exports, and deduct the value of imports.

(vii) Add undistributed profit of companies, income from government property and profits from public enterprises.

In India, the National Income Committee used the income method for adding up the net income arising from trade, transport, public administration, professional and liberal art, and domestic services. Under Indian conditions, due to lack of popularity of personal accounting practices, it is difficult to ascertain the personal income of individuals, the income method is not wholly practicable.

This method of estimating national income enables us to ascertain the share of each factors of production in the national income, and therefore, national income arrived under this method is known as nation income at factor cost. The great merit of this definition is that it shows the relative size of income received by different income groups such as landlord, capitalists, labour and entrepreneurs.

(iii) *Expenditure Method*

According to this method, the total expenditures incurred by the community of a country in a particular year are added to estimate the national income. The following are the expenditures to be taken into account for estimation of national income:

(i) *Personal consumption expenditure*: It is the expenditure by consumers on durable and non-durable consumption goods produced in the country during the year.

(ii) *Gross domestic private investment expenditure*: It is the expenditure by private entrepreneurs on replacements, renewals and new investments.

(iii) *Government's purchases goods and services*: It is the expenditure by the government of the country on consumption goods and capital goods.

(iv) *Net foreign investment*: The net foreign trade balance (exports minus imports).

This concept is based on the assumption that national income is equal to national expenditure.

To express it in symbolic terms:

$$Y = \Sigma (C + I + G) + [(X - M) + (R - P)]$$

where

C = Consumption Expenditure

I = Investment Expenditure, and

G = Government Purchases

1.2.5 Difficulties in the Estimation of National Income

Though all methods are used to calculate national income, yet the calculation is a complex affair and it has some conceptual and statistical difficulties. Prof. Simon Kuznets mentions the following difficulties:

(a) *Conceptual Difficulties*

The following are the conceptual difficulties found in calculation of national income:

(i) **Difficulty of Defining the Nation:** It is difficult to define the term 'nation' in the studies of national income. Whether the income earned by the nationals outsides the country is to be included or not is the difficulty while calculating national income. Therefore, the definition of nation goes beyond the political boundaries.

(ii) **Non-marked Services:** What kind of goods and servicees should be included or not in national income is the conceptual difficulty. Commodities and services having money value are included in the national income but there are goods and services which may have no corresponding flow of money payments. Services performed for love, kindness and mercy and not for money have an economic value but have no money value. The difficulty is whether these services should be included in national income and how to measure their money value. For example, a paid maidservant's services are included in the national income but later when she marries the master, she is not paid any more, though she continues to perform the same services, it is not included in the national income.

(iii) Choice of Method for Measuring National Income: There are three methods to measure the national income, viz. income method, product method and expenditure method. But it is difficult to choose any one method. For example, in countries like India both monetized and non-monetized sectors are existed side by side so it is difficult to use any one method. The use of the methods will be largely determined by the availability of statistics.

(iv) The Choice of Stage of Economic Activity: The production of goods and services passes several stages. It is difficult to decide what stage of economic activity has to be taken into account while calculating national income. It is agreed that any stage—production, consumption and distribution—may be adopted depending upon the function the national income estimate is expected to discharge. If the aim is to show the economic progress and power of the economy, then the production stage would be more suitable; if the aim is to measure the welfare of individuals, then consumption stage would be more useful.

(b) *Practical Difficulties*

The practical difficulties in estimating the national income are particularly great in underdeveloped countries of Asia and Africa. The main difficulties are as follows:

(i) Illegal Activities: Income earned through illegal activities such as gambling or illicit extraction of wine, etc. is not included in national income. Such goods and services do have value and meet the needs of the consumers. But by leaving them out, the national income works out to less than the actual.

(ii) Transfer Payments: Another difficulty in the calculation of national income is that of transfer payments which is associated with the income method of national income calculation. A person receives income of say ₹ 1000 per year, part of it may have been received as interest payment on government loans. This part is the nature of transfer payments and to be taken either as the income of the individual or of the government. If it figures under both the categories, aggregate national income will be unduly inflated. Therefore, the transfer of money from one person or group to another person or group should be avoided and the best way to solve this difficulty is to consider only the disposable income of individuals or groups, i.e. personal income minus all transfer payments.

(iii) Non-availability of Statistical Information: Another important difficulty is the non-availability of statistical material. This difficulty is not peculiar to underdeveloped countries, but even in advanced countries reliable and sufficient statistics are lacking. According to National Income Committee of India, the available statistics, especially for agriculture and small-scale industries, are extremely unreliable and incomplete.

(iv) Production for Self-consumption: Another difficulty most peculiar to backward countries is that a substantial part of the output is not exchanged for money in the market, it being either consumed directly by the producers or bartered for other goods and services in the unorganized sector. The existence of a vast unorganized and non-monetized sector makes calculation of national income very difficult.

(v) Multiple Occupations: There is little occupational specialization on the part of the people in underdeveloped countries. Many persons take up more than one activity to earn their livelihood. It becomes difficult to collect information about their incomes, etc. For example, the small farmers in India not only do farming, but also migrate to the industrial cities during the slack season to supplement their meager earning from agriculture.

(vi) Danger of Double Counting: The greatest difficulty in the calculation of national income is of double counting, which arises from the failure to distinguish properly between a final and intermediate product. There always exists the fear of a good or a service being included more than once.

If it so happens the national income would work out to be many times the actual. Flour used by a bakery is an intermediate product and that by a household the final product. To solve this difficulty, only the final goods and services are taken into account, and that is not so easy task.

(vii) Problem of Finding the Common Denominator: Another difficulty in calculating national income is that of price changes which fails to keep stable the measuring rod of money for national income. When price level in the country rises, the national income shows an increase even though the production might have fallen. On the contrary, with a fall in price level, the national income shows a decline even though the production might have gone up. Thus, the national income cannot be adequately measured under the conditions of price change. To solve this difficulty, the statisticians have introduced the concept of real national income, according to which the prices of the year in question are assessed in terms of prices of the base year.

(viii) **Capital Gains or Losses:** Capital gains or losses which accrue to property owners by increase or decrease in the market value of their capital assets or changes in demand are excluded from the GNP because such changes do not result from current economic activities. It is only when capital gains or losses are the result of the current flow or non flow of productive activities that they are included in the GNP.

1.2.6 Circular Flow of Income

The circular flow of income is the foundation stone of macroeconomics. The whole macroeconomics is built on the simple concept of circular flow of income. It provides the starting point for the study of different branches of macroeconomics. It discusses the flow of goods and services in the transactions between households and firms. The circular flow of income shows the interdependence between the different sectors of the economy. In short, it refers to a continuous circular movement of money and commodities within economy.

The modern economic life is characterized by a continuous circular flow of income. Households sell their productive services as factors of production to the firms and in return earn their income. In other words, firms' spending becomes households' income. Households buy the final goods and services produced from the firms. The total expenditure of households becomes income to the firms, which is equal to the value of final output of the firms. Values are created in productive areas of firms. All net value-added together determine the value of final output (GNP). The final output flows from the productive area of firms to the consumption area of households. It is shown in Fig. 1.1.

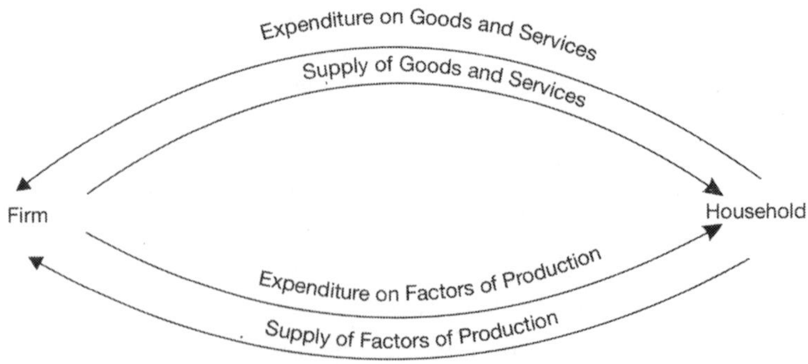

Fig. 1.1: Circular Flow of Income

An economy is divided into two sectors as household and firm to explain the circular flow of income. The household sector owns all the factors of production like land, labour, capital, etc. This sector receives income by selling its productive services to the firm. The firm produces goods and services to sell them to the household sector or consumers. Thus, the income of household is the expenditure of the firm and the income of the firm is the expenditure of the household. Hence, the income flows in a circular form between the household and firm that forms the circular flow of income.

1.2.7 Importance of the Study of National Income

The study of national income has the following importance:

(i) The national income study helps us to understand the structure of the economy. It tells us not only about the national income but also about the size of production and consumption, the level of taxation and saving and dependence of the economy upon foreign trade.

(ii) It throws the light on the relative importance of the different sectors of the economy. It tells us about the conditions of the production sector, the consumption sector, investment sector, the rest of the world sector and the other sectors.

(iii) It is a guide for the economic investigator. The national income data help them to analyze the behaviour of the economy. Such data are related to gross national product, government expenditure on goods and services, etc.

(iv) It helps the government to formulate new policies in response to changes in economic conditions in the country. There main function is to help the government to decide, guide or control economic conditions and to formulate economic policies to reduce poverty and inequalities.

(v) It helps the big business houses for assessing their performance and to improve their prospects on the basis of the statistical information about the various sectors of the economy.

(vi) The national income study is also useful for international purposes. A comparative study of a social accounts of the different countries of the world helps in the categorization of countries into underdeveloped, less developed and developed. It is on the basis of national income accounts that the various agencies of the United Nations make provisions for aid to poor countries of the world.

1.3 MODEL QUESTIONS

2-Marks Questions

1. Define macroeconomics.
2. What is macro static?
3. Write any two importances of macroeconomics.
4. Give any two of limitations macroeconomics.
5. Define national income.
6. What is GNP?
7. Name any two methods of national income calculation.
8. Mention any two difficulties of national income estimation.

(9) What do you mean by circular flow of income?

(10) Give any two importances of national income studies.

5-Marks Questions

1. Write a note on scope of macroeconomics.
2. State in brief the importance of macroeconomics.
3. Give a brief account of limitations of macroeconomics.
4. On the basis of the following data calculate national income by using product method:

Domestic output of all production sectors	= ₹ 10,000 cr
Depreciation charges	= ₹ 100 cr
Subsidies	= ₹ 1000 cr
Indirect taxes	= ₹ 1500 cr
Exports	= ₹ 2100 cr
Imports	= ₹ 2250 cr
Receipts from abroad	= ₹ 3100 cr
Payments made to abroad	= ₹ 2850 cr

5. Write a short note on difficulties of national income estimation.
6. State in brief the importance of national income studies.
7. Write a note on methods of national income calculation.
8. Give a brief account of circular flow of income.

10-Marks Questions

1. Define macroeconomics. Explain its scope and importance.
2. Define macroeconomics. Explain its importance and limitations.
3. Define national income. Explain its various concepts.
4. What is national income? Discuss the various methods of its estimation.
5. What are the methods of national income calculation? Discuss the various difficulties of its estimation.
6. Explain the meaning of national income and importance of its studies.

2

Classical Theory on Income and Employment

The economic welfare of the people is economic welfare of the nation. Higher the level of national income, higher will be the level of economic welfare. The national income of USA is higher so the people of USA enjoying higher standard of living. The national income of India is lower so the Indians are enjoying lower standard of living. Employment is the source of national income. The size of national output or national income depends upon the level of employment.

The Classical Theory of Employment deals with the determination of employment and solution to general unemployment problems.

The Classical Theory of Employment states that there is always full employment at equilibrium level in free capitalist economy. The general unemployment is not possible. The statement of the classical theory is based on J.B. Say's Law of Market.

Say's Law of Market states that the supply always creates its own demand. So there is equality between demand and supply. Thus, there is equality between income and expenditure and equality between savings and investment in the free capitalist economy.

An eminent classical economist A.C. Pigou introduced a modified version of the classical theory on employment. He introduced labour market in place of commodity market. He explained that the equilibrium between demand for and supply of labour determines wage rate which determines the level of employment in the economy.

The classicals admit that misbehaviour of the producers may create involuntary unemployment is short run temporarily. A.C. Pigou suggested wage-cut policy to solve such unemployment problems.

2.1 EMPLOYMENT

Economic welfare of the people of any country depends upon its national income. National income flows from various sources or occupations.

Employment is the source of national income. What is employment?

2.1.1 Meaning of Employment

In general sense, employment means job or work or occupation. But its meaning is little different in economics.

In economics, 'Employment' means the process that uses resources like man and materials, to produce goods and services in the economy. For example, tilling of the land to produce agricultural commodities.

It is very interesting fact for you to know 'what does determine employment'.

Since long back, many economists tried their best to answer this basic question. They placed various theories to explain the determination of employment and income. There are two well-known important theories on employment and income. These are (i) Classical Theory on Employment, and (ii) Keynes' Theory on Income and Employment.

2.1.2 Concepts of Employment

There are various concepts of employment used in economic literature. These are as follows:

(i) *Full Employment*

Full employment is an economic condition or situation where the unemployment is at a minimum and the number of unemployed persons is no greater than the number of vacancies.

In wider sense, 'Full Employment' is an economic situation where all the resources of the economy are fully utilized, except a few.

Every economy has a minimum level of unemployment of resources including human beings. The causal factors like technical changes, structural changes, etc. create unemployment problems temporarily. Such unemployment is found in every country but it is at a minimum level, i.e. 2 per cent of the labour force.

Except these minimum unemployed, all the resources including labour force are fully utilized to the extent of their productive capacity.

Full employment is also a phase of business cycle.

(ii) *Under Employment*

Under employment is an economic situation where the resources including labour are under utilized. In other words, it is an economic condition where the resources are not fully utilized to the extent of their productive capacity. For example, a weaver is capable to weave 100 feet cloth in 8 hours but we are using that weaver to weave only 50 feet cloth in 8 hours.

(iii) *Unemployment*

Unemployment is an economic condition where the resources including labour are not utilized. For example, there are workers who are not utilized.

In brief, a jobless situation is known as unemployment.

2.1.3 Types of Unemployment

There are various types of unemployment. These are generally classified into two types which are as follows:

(i) *Voluntary Unemployment*

There are jobs in the economy but the workers or persons are not ready to work. Such economic situation is called voluntary unemployment. For example, there are jobs in rural area but the people are not ready to work and they prefer to remain idle.

Whether to do job or not is depend upon person's willingness or psychology.

If a person remains willingly jobless or idle even though there is job for him, there will be no solution to such voluntary unemployment problem.

(ii) *Involuntary Unemployment:*

Involuntary unemployment is an economic situation of a country where people are ready to work but there are jobs to them. For example, in India 43 million persons are ready to do jobs but there are no jobs to them.

Involuntary unemployment is an economic problem. It affects adversely on the economic development of the country so it needs solution.

The employment theories tried their best to solve involuntary unemployment problem. For example, the Classical Theory of Employment suggested 'wage-cut policy' as solution to involuntary unemployment problem.

2.1.4 Types of Involuntary Unemployment

While studying involuntary unemployment, we generally face the following types:

(i) *Mass Unemployment*

The general deficiency of demand for goods and services leads to accumulation of unsold goods, decline in size of price and profits of some firms reduce the level of production and some other firms stop the production. It throws the workers out of employment. The large number of people became unemployed. Such unemployment is called mass unemployment. It is also known as 'Cyclical Unemployment' because generally at the time of depression, the large number of people becomes unemployed due to deficiency of demand.

(ii) *Frictional Unemployment*

The change in technology, changes in structure of the economy etc. are called frictions in the economy. The unemployment which is caused by the frictions or changes in the economy is called 'Frictional Unemployment'. There are two types of frictional unemployment. These are:

(a) **Structural Unemployment:** The structure of the economy consists of sectors like primary sector, secondary sector and tertiary sector. Any change in one sector leads to change in another sector. The unemployment created by structural changes is called 'Structural Unemployment'. For example, the decline in demand for agricultural goods may lead to increase in demand for industrial goods. So some people will become unemployed in agriculture. Of course, the industrial sector may create employment opportunities but the entire unemployed from agricultural sector cannot be absorbed fully; some of the people will remain unemployed.

(b) **Technical Unemployment:** The unemployment created by change in technology is called 'Technical Unemployment'. For example, computerization in banks has thrown some people out of employment.

(iii) *Seasonal Unemployment*

The demand for some goods and services depends upon seasons. For example, there is demand for woolen clothes in winter season. Similarly, there are certain goods produced in certain seasons. For example, sugar factories undertake production during sugar-cane cut-off season. During off season, such industries will remain closed and the workers of these industries will remain unemployed.

The unemployment created due to change in season is called 'Seasonal Unemployment'.

(iv) *Residual Unemployment*

The physical disablement, mental disablement, accidents, etc. create unemployment problems. The unemployment created by causal factors like physical or mental disablement and other than above reasons is called 'Residual Unemployment'.

The frictional unemployment is not a worried problem because it can be solved automatically through adjustments in long-run.

2.2 CLASSICAL THEORY OF EMPLOYMENT

Adam Smith, David Ricardo, J.S. Mill, J.B. Say, Edgeworth and A.C. Pigou are the eminent classical economists who propounded the theory on income and employment. So the theory is called 'The Classical Theory of Employment'. The Classical Theory explains about determination of employment and income levels and solution to general or involuntary unemployment problem.

2.2.1 Objectives

The classical theory of employment has the following objectives to explain:

(i) In free capitalist economy, the free play of economic forces itself brings about the fuller utilization of economic resources including labour or full employment.

(ii) There is always full employment at equilibrium in free capitalist economy. Thus, there is no general or involuntary unemployment.

(iii) The misbehaviour of the producers may generally cause over production which eventually results into general unemployment, temporarily in short-run. But it will be corrected through automatic adjustment between market forces in long-run.

(iv) Wage-cut policy corrects the general unemployment problem.

(v) The equilibrium between demand for and supply of labour determines wage-rate. The wage-rate determines level of employment and income in the economy.

2.2.2 Statement of the Theory

The classical theory of employment states that there is always full employment of labour and other resources in free capitalist economy.

The free play between market forces brings about equilibrium in long-run which results into full employment of labour and other resources. So there is no general or involuntary unemployment in the market economy. Any interference by the government or external forces with free play of economic forces shall fail to bring about full employment in market economy. Any lapses from full employment may result into creation of unemployment.

The classical believed that there is voluntary unemployment but there is no involuntary or general unemployment in market economy. If there is any general unemployment, that will be corrected through automatic adjustment between market forces in long-run. The general unemployment appears temporarily in short-run due to overproduction or technical changes. Such temporary general unemployment will be removed by the equilibrium between demand and supply forces in the long-run. Once again in long-run, the equilibrium full employment level will be restored and there will be no general unemployment in the market economy.

In brief, according to classicals, the equilibrium between demand and supply forces determines the level of employment and income in the market economy.

2.2.3 Assumptions

The classical theory of employment is based on several assumptions. They are discussed as under:

(i) *Assumption of Full Employment*

The classical theory assumes existence of full employment in free capitalist economy. According to classicals, there is no general or involuntary unemployment in free capitalist economy. But they admit that the incorrect calculation of producers may result into overproduction. The overproduction may create general unemployment problem in short-run. Such general unemployment is temporary and it will be corrected through automatic adjustment by market forces in long-run. The price mechanism takes the economy to equilibrium position in long-run. So there will be equality between demand and supply, income and expenditure and savings and investment.

(ii) *Assumption of Say's Law of Market*

Assumption of full employment is justified by Say's Law of Market.

Say's Law of Market states that the supply always creates its own demand. It means the production of goods generates income on the one side and supply equal worth goods on the other side. Since income is the source of demand, there is equality between demand and supply. Thus, supply creates its own demand. Whatever income is generated will be spent on consumption and investment. So there is equality between income and expenditure. Therefore, there is no general unemployment in free capitalist economy. It is based on the postulation that one's income is another's expenditure.

(iii) *Assumption of Built-in Flexibility*

The classical theory assumes the flexibility of wage rate, flexibility of interest rate, flexibility of price, etc. in capitalist economy.

The theory assumes that the wage-rate should be flexible to change in demand for labour and supply of labour conditions. Any deviation from equilibrium wage-rate should be corrected through demand for and supply of labour and equilibrium wage-rate should be restored.

Similarly, the interest rate and price of goods should be flexible to change in demand and supply conditions.

(iv) *Assumption of Automatic Adjustment*

The classical theory assumes the free market price system. The demand for and supply of goods determines the equilibrium price.

Any deviation from equilibrium price will be corrected through automatic adjustment between demand and supply and equilibrium price or rate will be restored.

(v) *Assumption of Perfect Competition in Labour and Product Markets*

Both labour and product markets should be perfect competitive markets.

(vi) *Assumption of Given Technology*

The classical theory assumes that there should not be change in technology in short-run.

2.2.4 A.C. Pigou's Modification

A.C. Pigou propounded the 'Classical Theory of Employment' in modified version. Pigou introduced labour market in place of commodity market. Pigou said that the equilibrium between demand for labour and supply of labour determines the wage-rate which provided employment to all workers in the labour market.

According to Pigou, there is no involuntary unemployment in free capitalist economy. The equilibrium between demand for labour and supply of labour brings about the full employment in free capitalist economy. Further Pigou suggested 'Flexible Wage Policy' to maintain equilibrium level full employment in the perfect competitive market economy.

Pigou also admitted that there is frictional unemployment in the market economy due to the reasons like overproduction, misbehaviour of the producers or technical changes. Such frictional unemployment is temporary. Pigou suggested wage-cut policy to correct the frictional or involuntary unemployment problem.

Pigou said that there are two types of wage, namely (a) Money wage (MW), and (b) Real wage (RW) and there is relation between 'Money wage' and 'Real wage'.

According to Pigou, the determination of the level of output, income and employment depends upon the conditions of demand for labour and supply of labour.

The demand for labour depends upon the 'Marginal Revenue Productivity of Labour' (MRPL). The marginal revenue productivity of labour is the sum of the product of 'Marginal Physical Productivity of Labour' (MPPL) multiplied by price of the output or commodity (P). It can be expressed algebraically as:

$$DL = f(MRPL) = f(MPPL \times P)$$

where DL = Demand for Labour

F = Functional Relation

MRPL = Marginal Revenue Productivity of Labour

MPPL = Marginal Physical Productivity of Labour

P = Price of output or commodity

There is opposite relation between MPPL and money wage rate. Higher the money wage rate; lower will be the MPPL.

Similarly, there is opposite relation between demand for labour and MPPL. As the demand for labour increases, the MPPL will fall..,

Pigou further said that the demand for labour (DL), money wage rate (MW) and MRPL or MPPL × P are equal to each other. It is expressed algebraically as:

$$DL = MW = MRPL = MPPL \times P.$$

According to Pigou, the demand for labour increases only when either the money wage rate declines or the price of commodity increases. Hence, Pigou suggested that either the money wage rate should be declined or the price of the commodity should be increased to solve the involuntary or frictional unemployment problem.

Pigou further explained that the money wage rate and price of the commodity determine the 'Real Wage' (RW). It can be written as:

RW = MW/P

where RW = Real Wage

MW = Money Wage Rate

P = Price of the Commodity

There is opposite relation between demand for labour and money wage rate or real wage. Increase in money wage rate or real wage leads to decline in demand for labour which creates involuntary unemployment in the capitalist economy. On the contrary, the decline in money wage rate or real wage leads to increase in demand for labour which solves the unemployment problem.

Money wage rate can be reduced directly but real wage can be reduced either by reducing money wage rate or by increasing price level. The price level depends upon the quantity of money and the volume of transactions ($MV = PT \therefore P = MP/T$). The price level will be increased or decreased by increasing or decreasing the quantity of money.

In brief, according to Pigou's version, the equilibrium between the demand for labour and supply of labour determines the wage rate which determines the full employment level of income and employment in free capitalist market. Wage-cut policy can be used to remove the involuntary unemployment.

2.2.5 Illustration of the Classical Theory

The equilibrium between demand for goods and supply of goods determines the full employment level of income and employment in market economy. So there is always full employment in free capitalist economy. Any lapse from equilibrium level of full employment, it will be corrected through automatic adjustment between market forces.

Pigou introduced labour market in place of commodity market. He explained that the equilibrium between demand for and supply of labour brings about equilibrium level of full employment. If any frictional or involuntary unemployment appears in short-run, that will be remove by wage-cut policy.

Pigou version of the theory of employment is illustrated in Fig. 2.1.

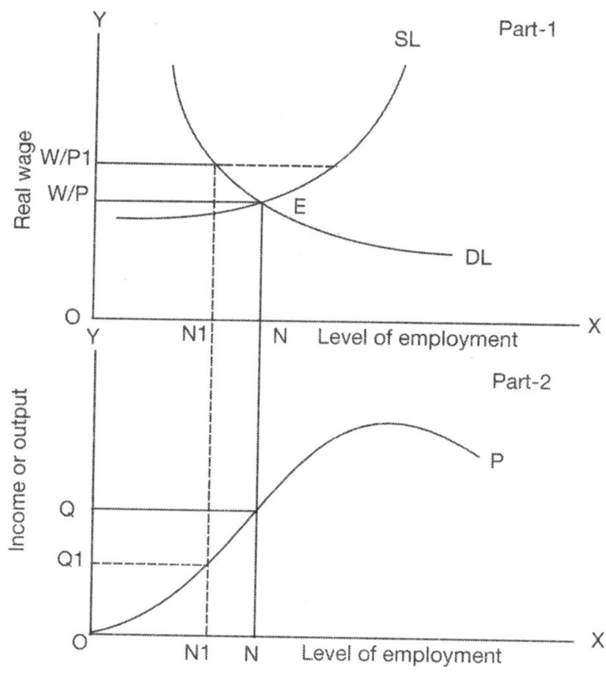

Fig. 2.1: The Classical Theory of Employment

Part-1

Part-1 of the figure explains the determination of equilibrium level of full employment.

OX axis measures the level employment. OY axis measures the real wage (W/P). SL curve represents the supply of labour. DL curve represents the demand for labour. DL and SL curves intersect each other at E point. The demand for and supply of labour are equal to each other at E point. It is the equilibrium point. The equilibrium determines the real wage OW/P and the level of employment ON. It is the equilibrium level of full employment.

Part-2

Part-2 of the figure explains the direct relation between employment and level of output or income. OX axis measures the level of employment. OY axis measures the level of output or income. At the equilibrium real wage W/P, the level of employment is ON and the level of output or income is OQ. The direct relation between employment and output or income is shown by OP curve.

Assuming that at W/P, real wage rate, the demand for labour is ON1 thus the level of involuntary unemployment is N1N. At ON1 level of employment or demand for labour, the level of output or income will be OQ1. To remove unemployment, Pigou suggested cutting the real wage by W/P1W/P. When real wage rate reduced, from W/P1 to W/P, the demand for labour or level of employment will increase by N1N thus unemployment will be removed. The reduction in real wage rate also increases the level of output or income by Q1Q.

In brief, according to the classical theory the aquarium, between demand for and supply of labour determines the size of income or output and employment. It brings about the full employment in market economy. Any deviation from equilibrium will lead to involuntary unemployment. Wage-cut policy can be used the remove involuntary or frictional unemployment.

The flexible wage policy or the flexible price policy helps the market forces to restore the equilibrium from any deviations and brings about the full employment in the market economy.

2.3 CRITICISMS

The eminent British Economist J.M. Keynes deviated from the classical thoughts since the publication of his book *The General Theory of Employment, Interest and Money* in 1936. He criticized the classical theory on employment on several grounds. Later the Keynesians also attacked on the classical employment theory. J.M. Keynes and his followers criticized the classical employment theory as under:

(i) *The Assumption of Say's Law of Market is Criticized*

Say's Law of Market believed that at the equilibrium level of full employment there are three equalities. They are:

(a) Demand (D) = Supply (S)

(b) Income (Y) = Expenditure (Y)

(c) Savings (S) = Investment (I)

Since the entire saving will be spent on investment, the income equal to the expenditure. Thus, the demand equals with supply.

Income (Y) is equal to the sum total of the expenditure on consumption (C) and the savings (S).

Thus, the 'Income Equation' can be written as $Y = C + S$.

On the other hand, the expenditure (Y) is equal to the sum total of the expenditure on consumption (C) and the expenditure on investment (I). Thus, 'Expenditure Equation' can be written as $Y = C + I$.

By substituting the value of Y in 'Income Equation' into the value of Y in 'Expenditure Equation', we get;

$$\begin{aligned} Y &= C + S \\ C + I &= C + S \\ I &= S \end{aligned}$$

Thus, there is equality between income and expenditure, savings and investment and demand and supply.

But Keynes said that the equality between savings and investment is invalid because the savings come from one group of the society and the investment is done by the other group of the same society. So, there is no equality between savings and investment ($S \neq I$). Therefore, income is not equal to expenditure and demand is not equal to supply. Thus, the very assumption of Say's Law of Market is invalid.

According to Keynes, the full employment is a rare concept. It is likely to be happening in long-run. It is like tomorrow that never comes and tomorrow we all are dead. So the existence of full employment is unrealistic assumption.

Further Keynes said that the equilibrium between economic forces does not mean the existence of full employment because such equilibrium may happen even before full employment situation. Thus, the classical theory is based on unrealistic assumption.

(ii) *Wage-cut Policy is Criticized*

Keynes criticized wage-cut policy as unfavourable measure. According to Keynes, wage-cut reduces the purchasing power of the people. It reduces the size of effective demand. Since effective demand is the determinant of the level of employment, the decline in effective demand creates still more unemployment and makes the unemployment problem still more worst. Therefore, wage-cut policy cannot remove or solve unemployment problem.

(iii) *Wage-cut Policy is Unacceptable*

The wage-cut policy affects adversely on socio-economic position of the people. Specifically, the wage-cut is opposed by the trade unions as well as the government.

(iv) *The Classical Theory Failed to Face 1930s 'Great Depression'*

The classical theory also advocates the interest rate flexibility as a measure to remove or solve unemployment problem. The central banks in European countries reduced the bank rate to the lowest level that is 2 per cent to encourage investment activities during Great Depression. But the countries failed to recover from Great Depression, because the low rate of interest failed to encourage investment activities. It is utter failure of the classical theory.

(v) *The Classical Theory Becomes Invalid in Short-run*

The classical theory is based on the strong belief that the investment (I) is the function of rate of invest (r). It can be written as: I = f (f). Keynes attacked on the classical theory on the rate of interest. Keynes said that investment (I) is the function of rate of interest (r) and marginal efficiency of capital (MEC). It is written as: I = f (r, MEC).

Further Keynes argued that the rate of interest remains unchanged in short-run because the rate of interest policy of central bank and lending policy of commercial banks remain stable.

Thus, the classical theory is inapplicable in short-run.

(vi) *The Classical Theory of Employment is Applicable Only to Free Capitalist Economy*

The classical assume free capitalist economy. But under modern context, the economies in one or the other way are controlled by the government or its monetary authorities. Thus, the classical theory does not applicable to modern economies.

(vii) *The Classical Theory is Based on Unrealistic Assumptions*

Assumptions like free trade or laissez-faire policy, perfect competition, constant technology are unrealistic. Now the modern economies have followed protectionist and liberal trade policy. The present markets are monopolistic competitive markets. The technology is changeable in long-run as well as in short-run. Thus, the theory is based on unrealistic assumptions.

2.4 SAY'S LAW OF MARKET

A French Economist J.B. Say (1767-1833), propounded the Law of Market in his book *Traite d' Economique Politique* in English which means *Treatise on Political Economy.*

The classical theory of employment is based on J.B. Say's Law of Market which states "Supply always creates its own demand".

Say assumed perfect competitive commodity market to explain the statement of the law of market. He believed that the general overproduction and general unemployment are not possible in free capitalist economy, because whatever the quantity of output is produced and supplied will be purchased or demanded. Thus, there is no question of general overproduction and general unemployment.

Say further explained that the main source of demand for commodity is the factor income generated from the process of production of the commodity itself. So the demand for the commodity will be created equivalent to the supply of the commodity produced by a production process. In other words, the production of commodity generates on the one hand, the supply of commodity and on the other hand, it generates equal value factor income or purchasing power to purchase or demand that commodity. So there is no surplus output or overproduction.

Similarly, there are no leakages to income stream, because whatever income is generated will be spent on consumption and investment. Whatever the income is saved will entirely be spent on investment. Thus, there is equality between income and expenditure, savings and investment, and demand and supply.

These equalities can be ascertained by the following equations:

Equation 1: Income Equation = $Y = C + S$

Equation 2: Expenditure Equation = $Y = C + I$

Here, Y = Income
C = Consumption
S = Savings
I = Investment

Income equation shows that the income is equal to the sum of expenditure on consumption and amount of savings.

Expenditure equation shows that the income is equal to the sum of spending on consumption and investment.

When we substitute the value of Y from income equation to the value of Y from expenditure equation, we will get;

$$C + I = C + S$$
$$I = S$$

It implies that the entire savings is spent on investment.

Since income is source of demand and production is source of supply, there is equality between demand and supply.

Dudley Dillard in his book *The Economics of J.M. Keynes* rightly says "Since saving is another form of spending, according to the classical theory, all income is spent, partly for consumption, partly for investment. There is no reason to expect a break in the flow of income-stream and therefore supply creates its own demand.

The statement of Say's Law of Market can be understood with the help of the following chart:

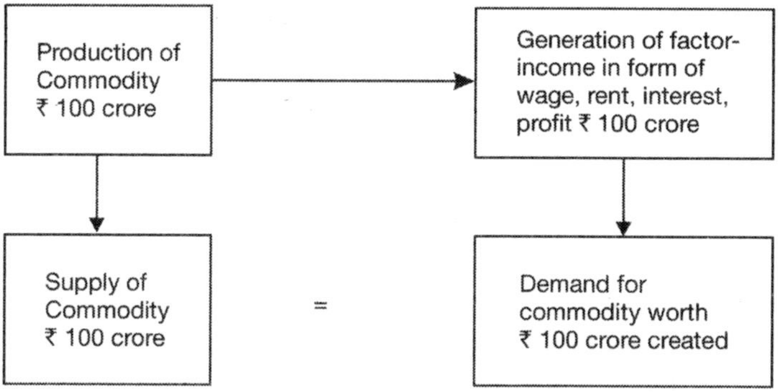

The chart shows that the production of commodity worth ₹ 100 crore on the one hand supplies commodity worth ₹ 100 crore and on the other hand it generates factor-income in form of wages, interest, rent and profit worth ₹ 100 crore. The factor-income ₹ 100 crore creates demand for commodity worth ₹ 100 crore. Thus, supply creates its own demand.

2.4.1 Implications

The important implications of Say's Law of Market are as follows:

(i) There is automatic adjustment between demand and supply. For example, if supply of commodity increases, the demand for commodity also increases. There is no government interference.

(ii) There is no overproduction. As the production increases, the factor-income will also increase. The increase in income raises the demand for commodity. Whatever is produced will be demand thus there is no over- production.

(iii) There is no general unemployment. Since there is no overproduction in free capitalist economy, the general unemployment is impossible. Even if the general unemployment appears, it will be temporary and it disappears in long-run due to automatic adjustment between market forces.

(iv) The employment of unemployed resources and labour will increase the production of goods.

(v) The free capitalist economy has 'built in flexibility'. There is no interference of the government and external forces. The economic system works automatically. For example, wage-rate changes according to charges in demand for and supply of labour conditions.

2.4.2 Criticisms

Say's Law of Market has been criticized on two different points of view:

(i) From production point of view, supply does not create its own demand. It is because the people cannot spend their entire income on goods. Same part of income will be saved. Thus, saving reduces the demand for goods which results into overproduction in community.

(ii) From employment point of view, supply of labour does not automatically adjust to its demand.

2.5 MODEL QUESTIONS

2-Marks Questions

1. What is employment?
2. What do you mean by involuntary unemployment?
3. Mention any two types of involuntary unemployment.
4. Mention any two types of unemployment.
5. Mention the central theme of classical theory of income and employment.
6. State the Say's Law of Market.
7. Mention any two assumptions of classical theory of income and employment.
8. What is the central theme of Pigou's wage-cut policy?
9. State any two criticisms on the classical theory of income and employment.
10. Mention any two implications of Say's Law of Market.

5-Marks Questions

1. Write a note on types of unemployment.
2. Write a note on A.C. Pigou's modification of classical theory on income and employment.
3. Mention the assumptions of the classical theory on income and employment.
4. Write a short-note on Say's Law of Market.
5. Write a brief account on the criticisms against the classical theory on income and employment.

10-Marks Questions

1. What is unemployment? Explain its various types.
2. Critically examine the classical theory on income and employment.
3. Discuss in detail Say's Law of Market.

3

Keynesian Economics

3.1. KEYNES' THEORY OF INCOME AND EMPLOYMENT

The classical theory of employment utterly failed to recover the economies from 1930s Great Depression. The classical theories failed to find out the solutions to great dispersion affected economies.

Keynes published his book *General Theory of Employment, Interest and Money* in 1936. He deviated from classical economic ideas and propounded new economic theories. Keynes' new economic theories are the new milestones in the world of economic doctrines. It created new economic waves. He brought importance to the 'Macroeconomic Analysis'.

In his book *General Theory of Employment, Interest and Money*, Keynes suggested the depression-affected countries to use 'Principle of Deficit Financing' as a method to recover from Great Depression. Keynes in his studies revealed that the deficiency of effective demand is cause for Great Depression. Under the principle of deficit financing, the government should increase the effective demand through deficit budget to solve general unemployment problem as well as to recover the economies from depression.

Hence, Keynes advocated that the effective demand determines the level of income and employment in the capitalist economy. He assigned key role to the government to regulate effective demand in the capitalist economy.

3.1.1 Relation between Output, Income and Employment

Before explanation of Keynes' Income and Employment theory, it is essential you to know the relation between output, income and employment in the economy. Keynes has taken into account the aggregate output, the aggregate income and the aggregate employment in the economy or community or country.

Keynes explained that there is a direct relation between output or income and employment.

The output depends upon the producing capacity of the economy. Labour force and marginal productivity of labour determine the producing capacity of the economy. It can be expressed in form of equation as:

$$Q = NXP \qquad ...(1)$$

where Q = Producing Capacity of the Economy

N = Labour Force in the Economy

P = Marginal Productivity of Labour

Higher the producing capacity, higher will be the level of output in the economy. For example, if the producing capacity of an economy increased from 100 million tones of output per annum to 200 million tones, the level of output will also increase from 100 million tones to 200 million tones per annum.

The supply of labour force depends upon the size of population and its quality. Higher the quantity and quality of the population, higher will be the supply of labour force.

The marginal productivity of labour depends upon three factors, namely (i) availability of natural resources, (ii) stock of capital and (iii) level of technology. It is expressed in form of equation as:

$$P = f(LKT) \qquad ...(2)$$

where P = Marginal Productivity of Labour

f = Functional Relation

L = Availability Natural Resources

K = Capital Stock

T = Level of Technology

The Equation (2) states that marginal productivity of labour is the outcome of available natural resources, capital stock and level of technology.

Since output depends upon producing capacity, the actual real output is equal to the producing capacity. Thus, it is expressed in the form of equation as:

$$Y = Q \quad \text{...(3)}$$

where Y = Actual Real Output

Q = Producing Capacity of the Economy

Since Q depends upon N and P, the actual real output is equal to the product of NXP. So it is expressed in form of equation as:

$$Y = NXP \quad \text{...(4)}$$

So there is a direct relation between output or income and employment because employment is the source of income. Therefore, this direct relation between income or output and employment is algebraically expressed as:

$$Y = f(n) \quad \text{...(5)}$$

Y = Income

f = Functional Relation

n = Level of Employment

Equation (5) expresses that income or output is the outcome level of employment.

Hence, Keynes advocated that there is a direct relation between output or income and employment. But he further said that the direct relation or proportion between the two depends upon time-element.

In short-run, the value of natural resources (L), capital stock (K) and level of technology (T) remains stable so there is close direct relation between income or output and employment. It is illustrated in Fig. 3.1.

OX axis measures the level of output, OY axis measures level of output/income. The proportion between output/income and employment is shown by OP curve. When employment is ON level, the level of output is OY. The increase in level of employment by NN1 leads to increase in level of output by YY1.

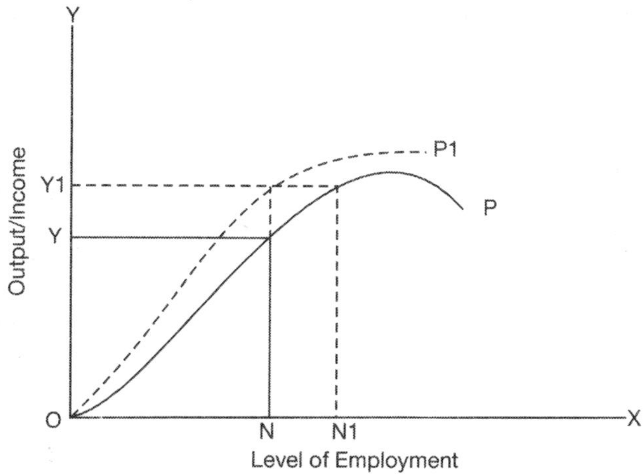

Fig. 3.1: Direct Relation between Output and Employment

In long-run, the value of L.K. and T may change, thus it may change the proportion between output/income and employment. For example, the improvement in level of technology may produce more by using same or less than before the amount of the labour force. It is shown by OP1 curve in Fig. 3.1.

3.1.2 Effective Demand

Keynes in his *General Theory* said that the 'Effective Demand' is an important determinant of employment. The deficiency of effective demand definitely results into creation of general unemployment in capitalist economy.

Keynes used employment as measure to calculate the total output or income of the economy. Thus, output is the source of employment. Algebraically, it is expressed as:

$$n = f(Y) \qquad \ldots(6)$$

where n = Employment

f = Functional Relation

Y = National Output or Income

The Equation (6) can be read as "employment is the resultant outcome of the national output or income".

The national output or income depends upon the effective demand. Higher the effective demand, higher will be the level of income and employment. Lower the effective demand, lower will be the level of income and employment.

The concept of effective demand is also found in Thomas Robert Malthus' theories but it is more systematically developed by Keynes.

The principle of effective demand is a very good contribution by Keynes to the theory of income and employment.

According to Keynes, 'effective demand' means the demand supported by ability to pay. In other words, the aggregate demand which is supported by aggregate supply of money income is known as 'Effective Demand'.

It is called effective demand because it effects on output or income and employment. In other words, effective demand determines the level of output or income and employment.

Increase in effective demand increases the size of output or income and employment Decrease in effective demand decreases the level of output or income and employment.

The deficiency of effective demand results into general unemployment in the capitalist economy.

'Effective Demand' depends upon aggregate demand and aggregate supply. The interaction or equilibrium between aggregate demand and aggregate supply determines the effective demand.

3.1.3 Aggregate Supply Function

It is also known as 'Aggregate Supply Price'. To Keynes, aggregate supply means the supply of income or supply of money value of goods and service.

Aggregate Supply Function (ASF) is a schedule of the various amounts of money which the entrepreneurs in an economy must receive from the sale of output at varying level of employment. At particular level of employment, the entrepreneurs must receive money income just equal to their cost. Thus, aggregate supply function represents the costs of the entrepreneurs in the economy.

The aggregate supply function is explained in Table 3.1.

Table 3.1: Aggregate Supply Function

Level of Employment (in lakh persons)	Aggregate Supply Function (Costs/money income in Crore)
100	500
150	1000
200	2000
250	2500
300	3000

As the level of employment increased from 100 lakh persons to 150 lakh persons, the costs or supply of money income increased from ₹ 500 crore to ₹ 1000 crore and so on.

As the level of employment decreases from 300 lakh persons to 100 lakh persons, the costs or supply of money income or aggregate supply decreases from ₹ 3000 crore to ₹ 500 crore.

The aggregate supply function explained in Table 3.1 is illustrated in Fig. 3.2.

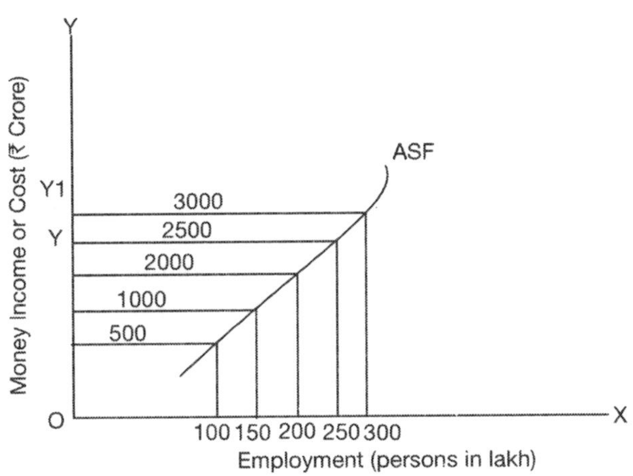

Fig. 3.2: Aggregate Supply Function Curve

Employment of persons in lakh is measured along OX axis. Supply of money income or cost in ₹ in crore is measured along OY axis ASF is the Aggregate Supply Curve. When employment of labour is 100 lakh persons, the supply of money income or cost is ₹ 500 crore. As level of employment increases to higher and higher level, the level of money income or cost will also increase higher and higher. It is shown in Fig. 3.1.

Aggregate supply is a determinant of effective demand.

3.1.4 Aggregate Demand Function

Aggregate demand is another important determinant of income and employment. It is also known as 'Aggregate Demand Price'.

Aggregate Demand Function (ADF) is a schedule of the various amounts of money which the entrepreneurs in an economy expect from the sale of their output at varying levels of employment. It represents the expected receipts or income which entrepreneurs receive by selling their output. The Aggregate Demand Function is explained in Table 3.2.

Table 3.2: Aggregate Demand Function

Level of Employment (Persons in lakh)	Aggregate Supply Function (Income or Receipts in ₹ in Crore)
100	1000
150	1500
200	2000
250	1500
300	1000

Aggregate demand shows expected income or receipts that the entrepreneurs may get by sell of their output at various level of employment. The entrepreneurs offer employment to 100 lakh persons when the expected sale-income is ₹ 1000 crore. They offer employment to 200 lakh persons when the expected sale-income is ₹ 2000 crore.

The sale-receipt or aggregate demand function also shows the spending on consumption and investment. The spending on consumption does not increase to the extent of increase in income. So the expected sale-receipts declined to ₹ 1500 crore and ₹ 1000 crore as employment increased to 250 lakh persons and 300 lakh persons respectively.

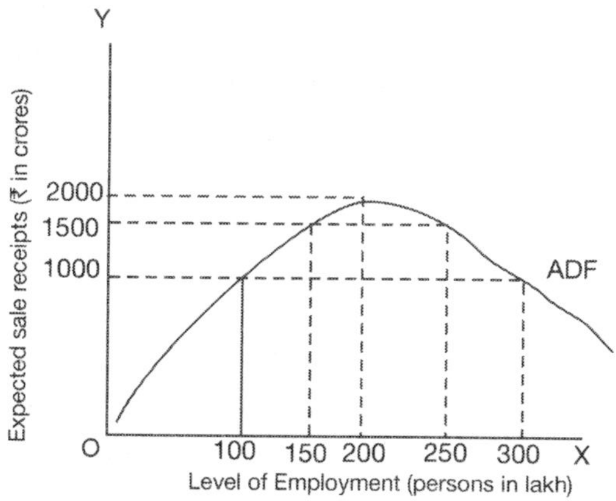

Fig. 3.3: Aggregate Demand Function Curve

The aggregate demand function which is explained in Table 3.2 is illustrated in Fig. 3.3.

Employment of labour in lakh persons is measured along OX axis. Expected sale-receipts in Rupees in crore are measured along OY axis. The expected sale-receipt of the entrepreneurs is the expenditure on consumption and investment by the community. ADF curve shows the aggregate demand.

Figure 3.3 explains the expected sale-receipts of the entrepreneur at various level of employment. The expected sale-receipt is ₹ 1000 crore when the level of employment is 100 lakh persons. The expected sale-receipts declined because the expenditure on consumption by the community did not increase to the extent of increased income.

3.1.5 Determination of Effective Demand

The equilibrium between the aggregate demand function and aggregate supply function determines the 'Effective Demand'. The determination of effective demand is explained in Table 3.3.

Table 3.3: Determination of Effective Demand

Employment (Persons in lakh)	Aggregate Demand Function (Receipts in ₹ in Crore)	Aggregate Supply Function (or Costs in ₹ in Crore)
100	1000	500
150	1500	1000
200	**2000**	**2000**
250	1500	2500
300	1000	3000

When the level of employment is 200 lakh persons, the aggregate demand and the aggregate supply are ₹ 2000 crore. Thus, at this employment level, both attained equilibrium or both are equal to each other. The entrepreneurs always seek that the expected sale-receipts or income should be equal to the actual money income or costs of their output. The equilibrium between aggregate demand and aggregate supply determined the 'Effective Demand' ₹ 2000 crore because at the equilibrium point the demand is supported by the ability to pay, i.e. ₹ 2000 crore money income of the community.

By using Table 3.3, the determination of effective demand is illustrated in Fig. 3.4.

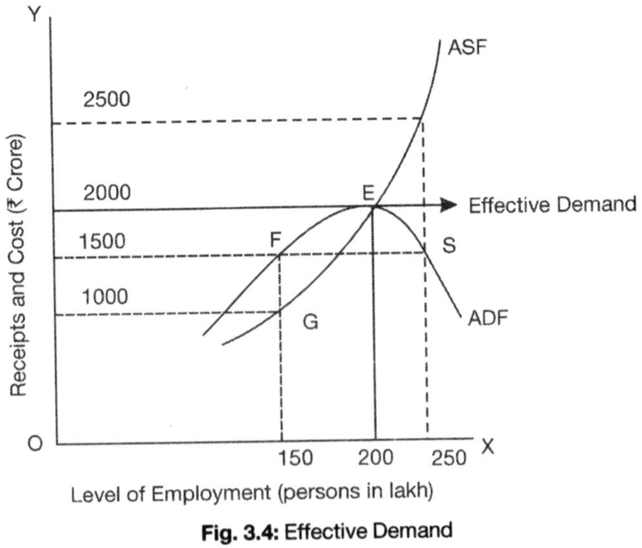

Fig. 3.4: Effective Demand

OX axis measures the level of employment in persons in lakh. OY axis measures the expected sale receipts or the actual costs. ASF curve shows Aggregate Supply Function and ADF curve shows Aggregate Demand Function.

In economy, the entrepreneurs offer different level of employment at different level of aggregate demand and aggregate supply. But they also seek to offer that level of employment where the expected sale-receipts of their output are equal to actual sale-receipts or cost of their output.

ADF and ASF cures are intersected each other at the point E and at that equilibrium point both are equal to each other. Thus, at equilibrium point E the Effective Demand is determined. At this equilibrium point, the level of employment is 200 lakh persons and both ADF and ASF are ₹ 2000 crore.

ADF and ASF are not equal to each other at any other points or level of employment other than the point E.

At the level of employment 150 lakh persons, ADF is ₹ 1500 crore which is shown by the point F on ADF curve. And ASF is ₹ 1000 crore which is shown by the point G on ASF curve. So ADF is greater than ASF. Here still more expected sale-receipts is possible by offering still more employment because the receipts are more than costs.

Similarly, at the level of employment 250 lakh persons, ADF is ₹ 1500 which is shown by the point S on ADF curve and ASF is ₹ 2500 crore which is shown by point K on ASF curve. So ADF is less than ASF. It means the receipts are less than costs at the level of employment of 250 lakh persons. Thus, no entrepreneurs offer employment to the community in loss.

In brief, according to Keynes, the equilibrium between aggregate demand and aggregate supply determines 'Effective Demand'. The effective demand represents the determination of level of employment and income or output.

3.1.6 Determination of Income and Employment

Keynes, in his *General Theory of Employment, Interest and Money*, explained that the aggregate demand and aggregate supply determine the effective demand and the effective demand determines the level of income and employment in capitalist economy.

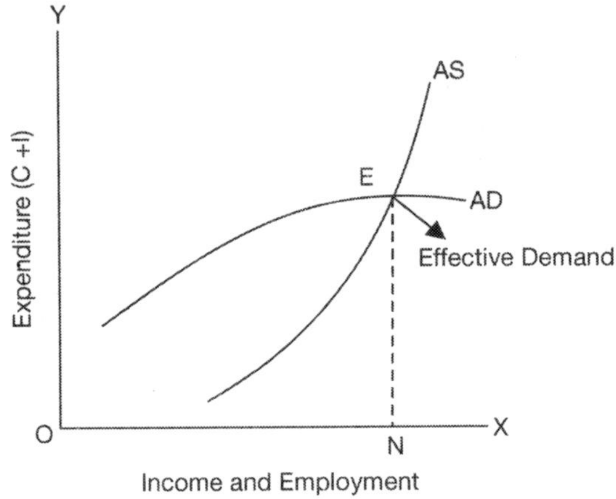

Fig. 3.5: Determination of Income and Employment

The equilibrium between aggregate demand and aggregate supply determines the effective demand. It is shown in Fig. 3.5.

OX axis measures income and employment while OY axis measures total expenditure on consumption and investment. AS is aggregate supply curve, AD is aggregate demand curve.

AS and AD curves are intersected each other at point E which is determined effective demand. When effective demand is at E the ON level of income and employment is determined in economy. Thus, the level of income and employment is determined in the capitalist economy.

Any change in aggregate demand and aggregate supply results into change in effective demand as well as change in level of income and employment. These changes are explained in Fig. 3.6.

The important points noted from Fig. 3.6 are as under:

(i) When aggregate demand curve is AD and aggregate supply curve is AS, the effective demand is E and the determined level of income and employment is ON.

(ii) Given the AS curve, the increase in aggregate demand shifts AD curve to AD1 which increases effective demand from E to E1 thus the level of income and employment increases by NN1.

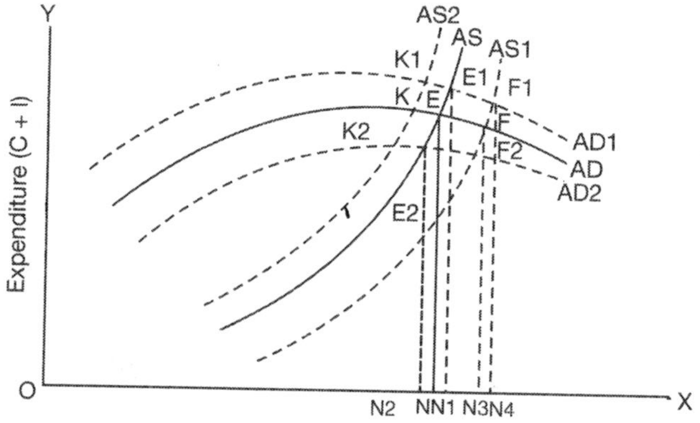

Fig. 3.6: Changes in AD and As Curves

(iii) Given AS curve, the declines in aggregate demand shifts AD curve to AD2, so the effective demand declines from E to E2 and so also the income and employment declined by NN2.

(iv) Given AD curve, the increase in aggregate supply shifts AS curve to AS1, the effective demand increases from E to F thus the level of income and employment increases by NN3 the decline in AS is shown by AS2 curve.

(v) AS1, AS2, AD1 and AD2 curves show change in aggregate supply and aggregate demand respectively. The resultant corresponding changes in effective demand are shown as E1E2, F1F2, K1 and K2 and changes in level of income and employment are shown as N1, N2, N3 and N4.

Keynes' explanation on aggregate supply and aggregate demand is as under:

(A) *Aggregate Supply*

To Keynes' aggregate supply (AS) means the supply of income or money value of total goods and services. It is expressed in the form of equation as:

$$AS = Y = C + S$$

where Y = Supply of Income
C = Consumption
S = Savings

The supply of income is equal to the sum of consumption expenditure and savings. For example, if the C=80 and S=20, then aggregate supply (AS) or supply of income (Y) is:

$$Y = 80+20=100$$
$$Y = 100$$

According to Keynes, aggregate supply depends upon (i) natural resources, (ii) level of technology, (iii) stock of capital and (iv) labour force or population. These are the determinants of aggregate supply. The developments and changes in these determinants of aggregate supply need long-time duration or long-run. Therefore, these determinants remain constant or unchanged in short-run. That is why Keynes said that the aggregate supply remain stable or constant in short-run. Thus, in short-run, aggregate demand plays important role to determine the level of income and employment.

(B) *Aggregate Demand*

To Keynes, aggregate demand (AD) means the total sum of the demand for consumer goods and demand for capital goods. Thus, it is expressed in the form of equation as:

$$AD = D = D_1+D_2$$

where D = Aggregate Demand
D_1 = Demand for Consumers Goods
D_2 = Demand for Capital Goods

D_1 and D_2 can be studies as:

(a) **Demand for Consumer's Goods (D_1):** It is also known as consumption and consumption expenditure which is denoted by C.

Keynes mentioned two types of consumption. They are: (1) autonomous consumption: It is denoted by a. It is not depended upon the level of income. The change in income does not influence on autonomous consumption. That is why it is called autonomous consumption.

The autonomous consumption depends upon the basic requirements of the community which do not depend upon the level of income. For example, food, shelter, etc.

(b) Induced Consumption: The consumption which is induced by the level of income is known as induced consumption. It is denoted by b(Y). For example, when the income increases from ₹ 100 to ₹ 200, the expenditure on consumption as result of it, increases from ₹ 80 to ₹ 120.

The autonomous consumption and induced consumption are shown in the Fig. 3.7.

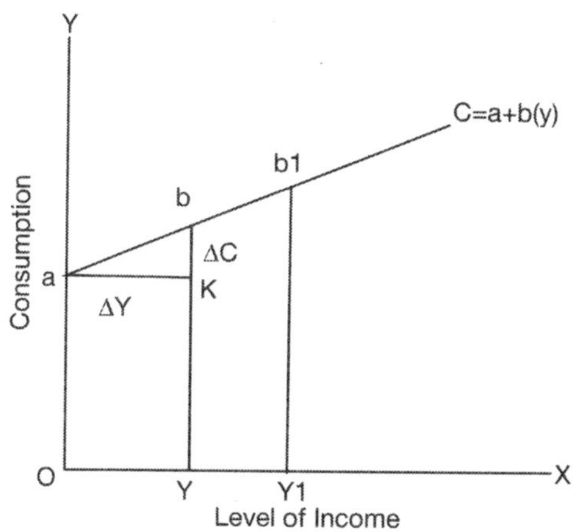

Fig. 3.7: Consumption Curve

OX axis measures the level of income OY axis measures the level of consumption. C is the consumption curve. Total consumption is the sum of autonomous consumption plus induced consumption. Therefore, it is expressed in the from of equation as:

C = a + b(y)

C = Total Consumption

a = Autonomous Consumption

b(y) = Induced Consumption

Y = Level of Income

b = Marginal Property to Consume (= $\Delta C/\Delta Y$)

For example, autonomous consumption is ₹ 30 and induced consumption is ₹ 50, so, the total consumption is C = a + b(Y), substitute the values,

$$C = ₹\ 30 + ₹\ 50 = ₹\ 80$$

The induced consumption [b(Y)] can be worked out as:

b = marginal property to consume
= $\Delta C/\Delta Y$
= increased consumption/increased income

If suppose increased consumption ₹ 50 and increased income is ₹ 100, the value of b or marginal property to consume will be:

$$b = C\Delta/\Delta Y = 50/100 = 1/2 \text{ or } 0.5$$

When we multiply b by y, we will get induced consumption. It can be calculated as:

Induced consumption = b(Y)
= 0.5(100)
= 0.5 × 100 = 50

In Fig. 3.7, when the income increased by OY (Y), the consumption increased from bK thus the increased consumption is:

$$bY - KY = bK\ (= \Delta C)$$

Therefore, $b = \Delta C/\Delta Y = bK/aK$

Thus, in our example b= bK/aK (=OY) = 50/100 = 1/2 or 0.5

Similarly, as the level of income increased to Y_1, the level of consumption increased to b_1Y_1.

Further Keynes explained that the level of consumption is depending upon level of income and marginal property to consume, algebraically it is written as:

C = f(Y, MPC)
where C = Consumption
f = Functional Relation
Y = Level of Income
MPC = Marginal Propensity to Consume

The functional relation between consumption and income is called 'Consumption Function'. Therefore, the consumption function is written as:

$$C = f(y)$$

The equation can be read as 'consumption is the resultant outcome of the level of income'.

According to Keynes, the value of marginal property to consume (c/y) determines the level of income and employment in the capitalist through 'multiplier effect'.

The consumption function depends upon various factors like govt. fiscal policy, corporate profit distribution policy, etc. These factors are classified as (i) Objective Factors and (ii) Subjective Factors.

According to Keynes, both subjective and objective factors remain constant or unchanged during short-run. Therefore, consumption function remains stable in short-run.

Hence, Keynes said that in short-run the 'Investment Function' plays important role to determine the level of income and employment.

(c) Demand for Capital Goods (D_2): It is also known as 'Investment' or 'Investment Expenditure'. Keynes explained that the investment depends upon rate of interest (r) and the marginal efficiency of capital (MEC). There is functional relation between investment and its determinants rate of interest and MEC. This functional relation is known as 'Investment Function' and it is expressed algebraically as:

$$I = f(r, MEC)$$

where I = Investment

f = Functional Relation

r = Rate of Interest

MEC = Marginal Efficiency of Capital

Keynes said that the lending policy of commercial banks and bank rate policy of central bank remain unchanged during short-run so the rate of interest remains unchanged in short-run. Therefore, investment depends only on MEC in short-run. Thus, 'investment function in short-run' can be written as

$$I = f(MEC)$$

The demand price of new capital goods or assets and the supply price of new capital goods or assets determine the value of MEC.

MEC is subject to fluctuations in short-run as it governs by business expectations.

Hence, Keynes explained that, in short-run, the MEC determines the level of investment, income and employment.

The fluctuations in MEC result into fluctuations in level of investment, income and employment in short-run in the capitalistic economy.

(d) Equilibrium between AD and AS: Keynes argued that the equilibrium between the aggregate demand (AD) and the aggregate supply (AS) determined the effective demand which determines level of income and employment in the capitalistic economy. It is shown in Fig. 3.8.

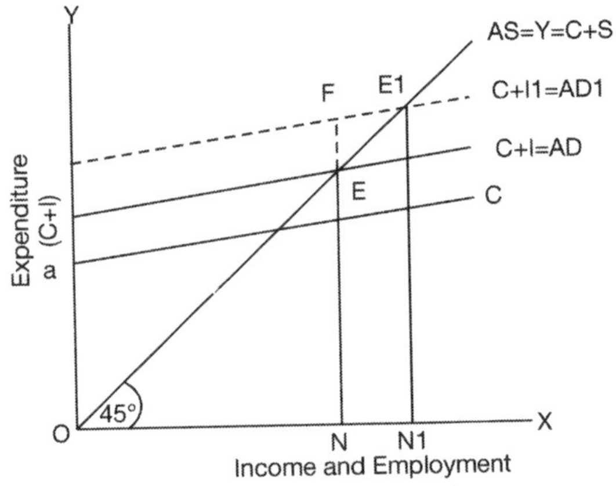

Fig. 3.8: Determination of Income and Employment

- OX axis measures the level of income and employment. Y axis measures the expenditure on consumption and investment.
- AS curve or 45° line represents aggregate supply which also represents the supply of income, i.e. Y=C+S.
- AD curve represents the expenditure on consumption and investment which is known as aggregate demand.

- AS and AD curves intersected each other at E which is called 'Effective Demand' which determined ON level of income and employment.
- When the expenditure on investment is increased by FE, the aggregate demand increased to AD1 (=C+I_1), the new equilibrium point is E_1 thus effective demand increased from E to E_1 so the level of income and employment increased to N_1. That is when AD or investment increased by FE, the level of income and employment increased by NN_1.
- In recent years, post-Keynesians added the 'Government Expenditure' (G) to the aggregate demand, i.e. AD=C+I+G.

3.1.7 Conditions of 'Full Employment'

Keynes argued that there are two conditions essential to attain full-employment level in capitalist economy. They are:

(i) Equilibrium between Aggregate Demand (AD) and Aggregate Supply (AS): It is one of the essential conditions to attain full employment level but it is not sufficient condition. According to Keynes, such equilibrium may take place even before the 'full-employment level'. It is illustrated in Fig. 3.9.

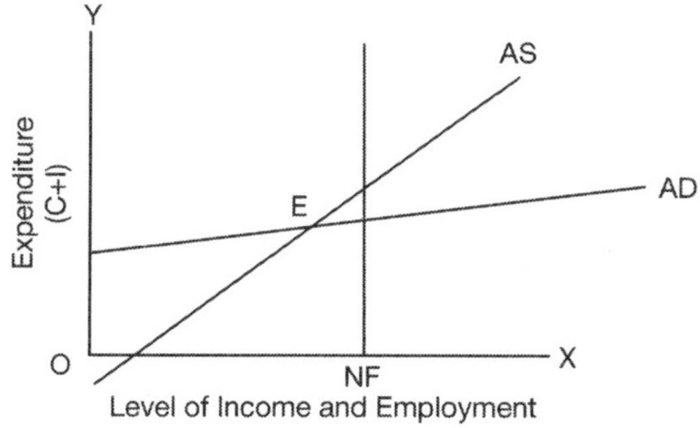

Fig. 3.9: Less than Full Employment Equilibrium

- NF is the line shows the full employment level income and employment.
- Point E shows the equilibrium between AD and AS. It is known as 'less than full employment equilibrium'.

(ii) Equilibrium between 'Planned Saving' (PS) and Planned Investment (PI): Keynes argued that the equilibrium between planned saving (PS) and planned investment (PI) is another essential condition to attain full employment level in the capitalist economy.

Any disequilibrium between PS and PI will result into change in the level of income and employment. For example, if planned saving exceeds planned investment, it will create more unemployment. Both the conditions of equilibrium full employment level are illustrated in Fig. 3.10.

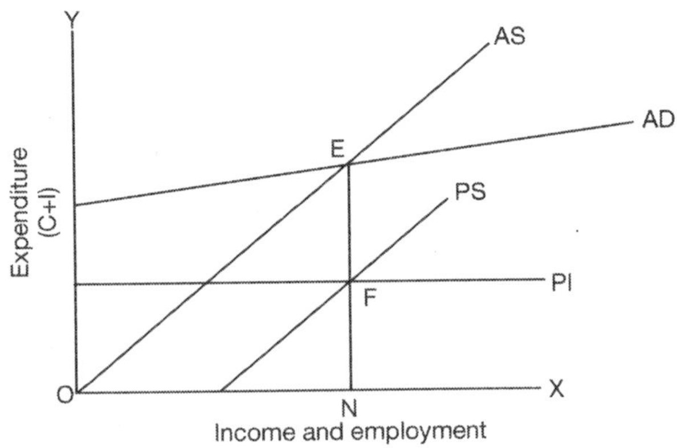

Fig. 3.10: Equilibrium Level of Full Employment

- AS is aggregate supply curve and AD is aggregate demand curve. Both are intersected each other at E so AS=AD at equilibrium point E.
- PS is planned saving curve and PI is planned investment curve. Both are intersected at F point so PS=PI at the equilibrium point F.
- ON is the full employment level of income and employment.

3.1.8 Summary

Keynes' theory of income and employment is summarized in the form of the following chart:

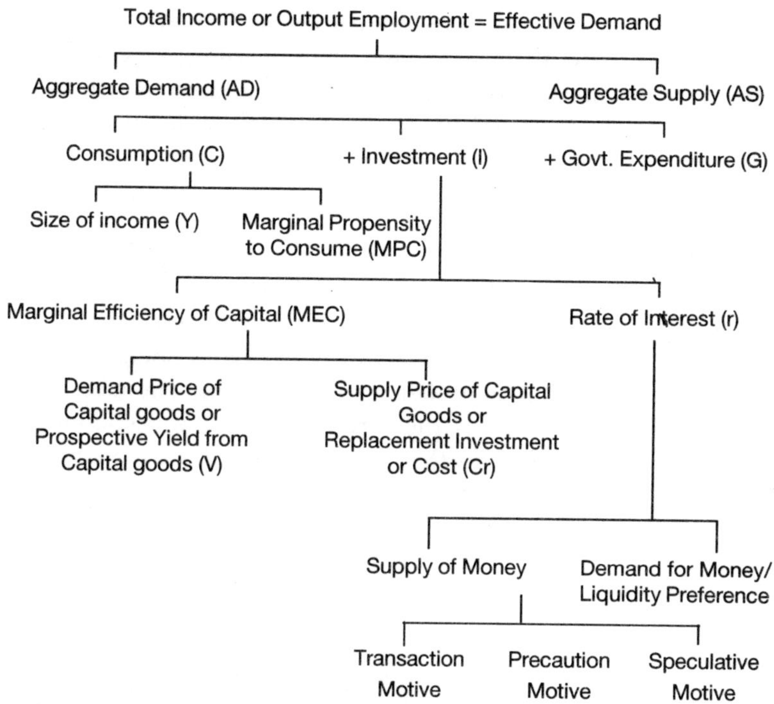

The equilibrium between aggregate demand and aggregate supply determines the level of income and employment in the capitalist economy. The aggregate demand consists of consumption, investment and government expenditure. The level of income and marginal propensity to consume determine the level of consumption. Rate of interest and marginal efficiency of capital determine the level of investment. The demand price and supply price of capital goods determine marginal efficiency of capital. Demand for money and supply of money determine the rate of interest.

In short-run, aggregate supply, consumption function and rate of interest remain constant thus, according to Keynes, the marginal efficiency of capital plays an important role in investment function which influences on aggregate demand and level of income and employment.

To Keynes, the deficiency of effective demand is the cause for general unemployment. Thus, Keynes suggested the government to undertake expenditure on public works and social security schemes. He argued that the government expenditure enhances the purchasing power of the community which raises the effective demand and so also the level of employment. Thus, the general unemployment problem will be solved.

Keynes gave more importance to aggregate demand.

3.1.9 Working of the Theory

Keynes suggested the government to use deficit financing to recover the economy from depression or deflation. The government expenditure on public works and social security schemes will inject new money into circulation. The increase in supply of money reduces the rate of interest and encourages investment activities. It further raises the aggregate demand and thus raises the level of income and employment. Thus, Keynes explains the working of income and employment theory. He also

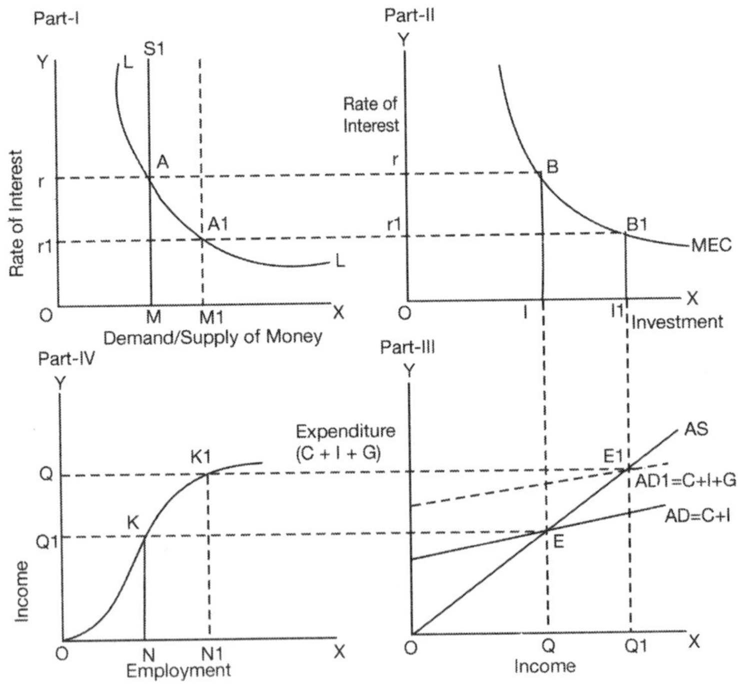

Fig. 3.11: Working of Keynes' Income and Employment Theory

explains the role of rate of interest in determination of income and employment.

The working of Keynes' income and employment theory is illustrated in the Fig. 3.10.

- Part-I explains the determination of rate of interest by equilibrium between demand for money and supply of money. LL Curve represents demand for money. SM curve represents supply of money. Both LL and SM curves are intersected each other at point A so determined rate of interest is or. OX axis measures demand for and supply of money and OY axis measures rate of interest.
- Part-II explains investment function. OX axis measures the level of investment, while OY axis measures rate of interest. MEC curve represents the marginal efficiency of capital and the relation among rate of interest, marginal efficiency of capital and level of investment. When rate of interest is or the marginal efficiency of capital is at B and the level of investment is OI.
- Part-III explains the determination of effective demand and so also the determination of the level of income in the capitalist economy. OX axis measures the expenditure (C+I+G). AS is aggregate supply curve and AD is aggregate demand curve (C+I). When the level of investment is OI, the intersection point between AS and AD is E, at effective demand E, the determined level of income is OQ.
- Part-IV explains the relation between level of income and the level of employment in the economy. OX axis measures the level of employment and OY axis measures income OP curve shows the direct relation between the level of income and employment. When the determined level of income is OQ, the level of employment is ON.

Under deficit finance, the increase in government expenditure, increased the supply of money to OM1, which is shown by S1M1 curve. It reduced the rate of interest to or1 which increased the investment to OI1 level. The increased government expenditure has increased the aggregate demand to AD1 (=C+I+G). It raised effective demand to E1 which raised the level of income to OQ1 and the level of employment to ON1. Thus, works the Keynes' Income and Employment Theory.

The theory also explains how to remove unemployment in the economy. Assuming that there is NN1 level of unemployment in the economy. To avoid unemployment, government undertook expenditure on public works which raised the supply of money by MM1 and reduced the rate of interest by rr1. The reduced rate of interest has increased the level of investment from AD to AD1 thus the effective demand increased to E1. The increase in effective demand raised the level of income by QQ1, and the level of employment is removed or solved.

The rate of interest played an important role in determination of income and employment in the economy.

3.1.10 Critical Appreciation

Keynes' Income and Employment Theory has definitely contributed new concepts and thoughts to the world of economic doctrines. The theory has theoretical and practical significance. But its failures and weaknesses cannot be ignored. So the critics criticized the theory on several grounds.

Keynes' Income and Employment Theory has been criticized as under:

(i) *Effective Only in Depression Economy*

Critics said that the Keynesian Income and Employment Theory is applicable to the depression economy. So it is not applicable to advanced countries that are facing inflation.

The follower of Keynes, Prof. Harris has defended the Keynesian theory from the criticism. Prof. Harris said that the Keynesian theory is applicable to both advanced countries and under-developed countries because the effective demand plays important role in both types of economies. So Keynes' theory is a general theory.

(ii) *Keynes' too has Capitalist View*

Critics said that Keynes has also stressed on profit motive. Keynes much stressed on marginal efficiency of capital (MEC) which is profit motive so Keynes' theory is not valid in socialist and communist countries.

The followers of Keynes also defended the theory from the criticism saying that even in socialist and community countries the resources are allocated on the basis of rate of return for best use. Thus, Keynes' theory is valid in all types of economies.

(iii) *Not a Sufficient Dynamic Theory*

According to critics, Keynes' theory is neither static theory nor dynamic theory but it is a comparative static theory. The theory simply compares one equilibrium situation to another equilibrium situation of the economy. It did not explain the movement from one point to another point of equilibrium.

(iv) *Theory Ignored Long-run*

Prof. F.A. Hayek criticized the Keynesian theory as a short-run analysis. Keynes too admitted that "we all are dead in long-run". So he argued to conçern with short-run problems. But Prof. Hayek said that Keynes' concern with short-run problems is a serious and dangerous intellectual error which may effect adversely on civilization. The economic planning, growth and development are long-run effects or concerns thus they should not be neglected.

(v) *Theory Ignored 'Micro Economic Analysis'*

Keynes used macro approach to explain his theory of employment. He took into account the aggregate demand, aggregate consumption, aggregate investment, etc. but he ignored micro approach. Modern economists argued that macro approach is incomplete without the use of micro approach. The integration of both approaches is necessary to study economic problems.

(vi) *Theory Ignored Principle of Acceleration*

Keynes argued that the investment multiplier theory is enough to explain the generation of income. But critics argued that the principle of acceleration is important tool to explain business cycles. The combined effect of investment multiplier and acceleration can help to study the magnitudes of business cycles.

(vii) *Theory Neglected Non-Monetary Factors*

Keynes' theory has considered only monetary factors. The critics said that the non-monetary factors like resources, labour force, technology, etc. which also influence on the generation of income and employment. It is neglected by Keynes.

(viii) *Keynes' Consumption Function is Criticized*

Keynes explained that the consumption is the resultant outcome of the level of income. But modern economy disagreed with Keynes' consumption function.

Prof. James Duesenbury argued that the current consumption (Ct) is the resultant outcome of both current income (Yt) and previous level of income (Yo) enjoyed by the community. He also considered demonstration effect on consumption.

Milton Friedman argued that the permanent consumption (Cp) varies with the variations in permanent income (Yp).

F. Modigliani argued that the consumption behavior differ from short-run to long-run. In short-run, the consumption-income relationship is non-proportional. In long-run, the consumption is a function of life time expected income of the consumer.

Prof. Henry Hazlitt criticized the Keynesian consumption function saying that it deals with mathematical relationship between consumption and income but does not explain the consumption tendency.

3.1.11 Superiorities of the Theory

Even though, Keynes' theory of income and employment has been criticized, it claims superiorities as under:

(i) It is theoretically sound: Keynes' theory on employment is free from assumptions so it is theoretically sound. It is based on macro thoughts. It helps to explain business fluctuations like inflation and deflation. The theory has very good theoretical framework.

(ii) Keynes proved with the help of his theory that the government interference in economic matters was in the interest of public and of the economy. Full employment cannot be brought automatically in the free market economy. It discards the argument of laissez faire policy of classical.

(iii) Keynes also proved that the deficit budget policy is the best policy to increase the level of income and employment. It discarded the balanced budget policy of classical.

(iv) Keynes gave importance to public works programme to fight against the depression or deflation. Modern governments have virtually accepted their programme.

(v) All economies or governments have adopted full employment policy. They design their budgets to achieve full employment.

Hence, it is admitted fact that the Keynes' income and employment theory has several superiorities. It is theoretically sound and practically important theory. Therefore, Keynes' theory is considered as 'General Theory'.

3.2 CONSUMPTION FUNCTION

Meaning

The level of consumption depends upon the level of income. So the functional relation between consumption and income is called 'consumption'. Thus, consumption function expresses the relationship between income (Y) and consumption (C).

According to Dernburg McDougall, the schedule that relates consumption to disposable income is called propensity to consumption function. In the words of R.G. Lipsey, "Consumption Function is nothing more than a statement of the relation between consumption expenditure and income". Thus, it can be mathematically expressed as:

$$C = f(Y)$$

where C = Consumption

Y = Income

f = Functional Relation

The functional relation between consumption and income can be understood with the help of consumption schedule.

Consumption Schedule

Consumption function is also known as 'Propensity to Consume'. It can be explained with the help of consumption schedule. The consumption schedule is a tabular statement showing the various levels of consumption at corresponding to different levels of income. A hypothetical consumption schedule is given in Table 3.4.

Table 3.4: Consumption Schedule

(₹ Crore)

Income (Y)	Consumption (C)
100	80
200	150
300	210

Table 3.4 shows that the level of consumption varies at various level of income. It also shows that when income increases from ₹ 100 crore to ₹ 200 and ₹ 300 crore, the level of consumption also increases from ₹ 80 crore to ₹ 150 and ₹ 210 crore. But the rate of change in consumption is less than the rate of change in income. It is also illustrated in Fig. 3.12.

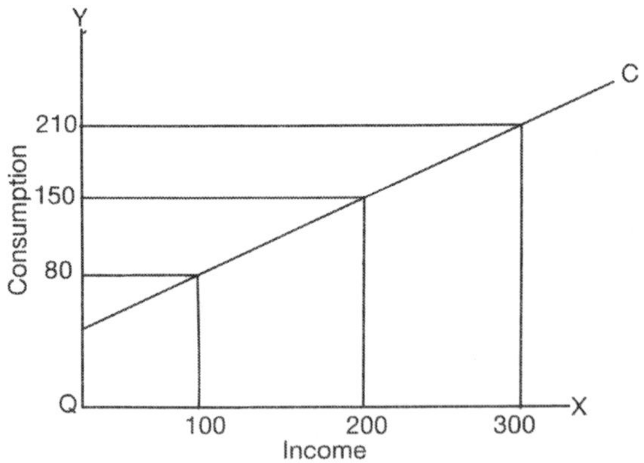

Fig. 3.12: Consumption Function

Income is measured along OX axis and consumption through OY axis. The C curve is a consumption curve that shows the functional relation between consumption and income.

3.2.1 Classical View

Classical economists thought that the level of consumption depends upon the rate of interest through level of savings. There is direct relation between rate of interest and savings. Further the level of consumption is oppositely related with savings: higher the savings lower will be the consumption and vice versa. A rise in the rate of interest induces the people to save more and thus reduce their level of consumption. According to classical writers, savings is a positive function of the rate of interest and therefore consumption is a negative function of rate of interest. Keynes does not accept this idea.

3.2.2 Keynes' View

Keynes disagrees with classical argument that consumption depends upon rate of interest through savings. He said that the rate of interest does not influence on rich people because already they have sufficient savings similarly it does not influence the poor people they have no savings at all. So according to Keynes, a major determinant of consumption is the level of disposable income.

Hence, the net influence of the rate of interest seems to be indeterminate. Ultimately, it is the level of income which determines consumption. Thus, Keynes expressed the consumption function in mathematical term as:

$$C = f(Y)$$

3.2.3 Keynes' Psychological Law of Consumption

Keynes propounded a basic law about the consumption function. This has been described as psychological law of consumption. Prof. Kurihar states Keynes' Psychological Law of Consumption as: when the aggregate income increases, consumption expenditure will increase but not to the extent of increase in income. It means that out of total increment in income, a part of it will remain unspent on consumption. Keynes argues that the entire increased income of the community cannot be spent on consumption because (i) the human wants are satiable and (ii) the application of law of diminishing marginal utility. For example, if the community income increases by 100 per cent, the consumption will increase by less than 100 per cent.

Propositions

Keynes' Psychological Law of Consumption depends on the three propositions:

(i) When income increases, consumption expenditure also increases but not to the extent of increase in income. It is expressed as:

$$\Delta C/\Delta Y < 1$$

(ii) The increased income will be divided in some proportion between consumption expenditure and saving. It follows from the above proposition when the entire increase in income is not spent on consumption and thus a part of that increased income is saved. It is expressed in form of equation as:

$$Y = C + S$$

(iii) Increase in income always leads to an increase in both consumption and saving. But the consumption cannot increase to the extent of income increases. So the savings also increases as the income increases. It is expressed as:

$$\Delta Y = \Delta C + \Delta S$$

With the help of the law and its three propositions the consumption function can be explained with the help of Table 3.5.

Table 3.5: Consumption Function

Income (Y)	Consumption (C)	Savings (S=Y–C) (₹ in crore)
0	20	–20
60	70	–10
120	120	0
180	170	10
240	220	20
300	270	30
360	320	40

According to Keynes there are two types of consumption, namely (i) autonomous consumption that does not depend upon the level of income (denoted as a) and (ii) induced consumption depends upon the level of income (denoted as b(Y)). So even at zero level of income there is consumption but the savings will be negative.

Later as income increased to ₹ 60 crore and so on, the consumption increased to ₹ 70 crore and so on the size of increase in consumption is less than the increase in size of income. For examine, the increase in income is ₹ 120 crore – ₹ 60 crore = ₹ 60 crore meanwhile its resultant increase in consumption is ₹ 70 crore – ₹ 20 crore = ₹ 50 crore so:

$$\Delta C/\Delta Y < 1 = ₹\ 50 \text{ crore}/ ₹\ 60 \text{ crore} = 5/6 = 0.83$$

Since increase in consumption is less than the increase in income, the savings increases as there is increase in income. For examine, when income increased from ₹ 120 crore to ₹ 180 crore i.e. by ₹ 60 crore, the consumption increased by ₹ 50 crore (₹ 170 crore – ₹ 120 crore = ₹ 50 crore) and the savings increased by ₹ 10 crore (₹ 10 crore – ₹ 00 crore = ₹ 10 crore). Hence,

$$\Delta Y = \Delta C + \Delta S$$

$$₹\ 60 \text{ crore} = ₹\ 50 \text{ crore} + ₹\ 10 \text{ crore}$$

In brief, the law states that there is functional relation between income and consumption and the consumption increases as income increases but less than it.

It can also be illustrated in Fig. 3.13.

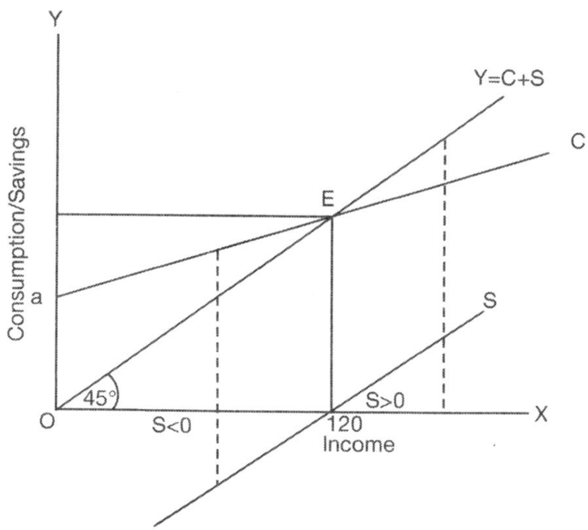

Fig. 3.13: Consumption Function

Income is measured along OX axis and consumption and savings are measured along OY axis. Y=C+S is the income line that shows supply of money income is equal to the sum of consumption-expenditure and savings or total expenditure. So it is shown by 45° line. Curve C shows consumption and curve S the savings. The income and consumption are equal to each other at point E_2 i.e. ₹ 120 crore = ₹ 120 crore, so savings is zero. To the right-side of E, income is more than consumption so the savings is positive (>0) and to the left-side of E, income is less than consumption so the savings is negative (<0). Oa is the size of autonomous consumption. Since the consumption consists of autonomous consumption, it is always positive (>0) so its curve starts from a. However, in brief, consumption is the functional out-come of the level of income.

Assumptions and Implications

Keynes psychological law of consumption is based on the following assumptions.

(i) It Assures a Constant Psychological and Institutional Complex: The law is based on the assumption that psychological and institutional factors influencing consumption expenditure remain constant. Such factors are income distribution, tastes, habits, social customs, price movements, population growth, etc. In the short-run, they do not change so the consumption depends on income alone. Thus, consumption function remains constant in short-run.

(ii) It Assumes the Existence of Normal Conditions: The law assumes normal conditions in the economy or country. There should not be any abnormal and extraordinary circumstances like war, revolution or hyper in inflation, etc. in the economy. Otherwise the law will not operate.

(iii) It Assumes the Existence of a Laissez-faire Capitalist Economy: The law operates in a free capitalist economy where there is no government intervention. All economic activities are free from central bank or government control.

Prof. Kurihar opines that "Keynes's law based on these assumptions may be regarded as a rough approximation to the actual macro behavior of free consumers in the normal short period".

Some Important Implications

The law has the following important implications:

(i) The law highlights the importance of consumption function. Keynes psychological law invalidates Say's law of market, viz. supply crates its own demand. It says that whatever is produced is not consumed entirely but some part it will remain unconsumed so there is no equality between demand and supply, income and expenditure and savings and investment.

(ii) The law also highlights that the marginal propensity to consume is always less than one so overproduction and unemployment appears in the free capitalist economy. Thus, there is need for government interference.

3.2.4 Functional Relation between Income and Consumption

Keynes considered consumption function or the functional relation between income and consumption in terms of average and marginal concepts as under:

(i) Average Propensity to Consume (APC) and Average Propensity to Save (APS): The average propensity to consume may be defined as the ratio of consumption expenditure to any particular level of income. In other words, it is consumption expenditure per unit of income. It is expressed in the following form:

$$\text{Average Propensity to Consume} = \frac{\text{Total Consumption}}{\text{Total Income}}$$

$$\text{APC} = \frac{C}{Y}$$

where C = Total Consumption of Community

Y = Total Income of Community

It is expressed as the proportion of consumption to income.

Keynes further argued that the entire income cannot be spent on consumption so some part of it would remain unspent which is called savings. The ratio or proportion of total savings to total income is called 'Average Propensity to Save'. It can be expressed as:

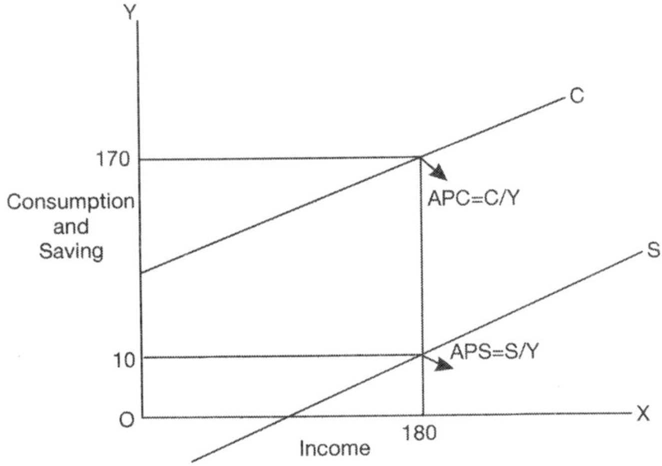

Fig. 3.14: APC and APS

$$\text{Average Propensity to Save} = \frac{\text{Total Saving}}{\text{Total Income}}$$

$$\text{APS} = \frac{S}{Y}$$

where S = Saving, Y = Income

Since Y = C + S means income is divided into consumption and savings, the total sum of APC and APS is equal to one. Thus, it can be written as:

$$\text{APC} + \text{APS} = 1$$

Similarly:

$$\text{APC} = 1 - \text{APS}$$

Or

$$\text{APS} = 1 - \text{APC}$$

For example, if the value of APS = ¼, find out the value of APC. By substituting the value of APS in the following equation, we can find out the value of APC as:

$$\text{APC} = 1 - \tfrac{1}{4} = \tfrac{3}{4}$$

APC and APS can also be illustrated in Fig. 3.14.

C is consumption curve and S the savings curve. In Fig. 3.14, the total income is 180, it is divided as 170 for consumption and 10 for savings so:

$$APC = C/Y = 170/180 = 0.94 \text{ and}$$

$$APS = S/Y = 10/180 = 0.06.$$

Therefore, $APC + APS = 1 = 0.94 + 0.06$

(ii) **Marginal Propensity to Consume (MPC) and Marginal Propensity to Save (MPS):** Further Keynes argued that the increment in income leads to increase in both consumption and savings.

"The ratio of change in consumption to the change in income is called Marginal Propensity to Consume". It can be expressed in the following formula:

$$\text{Marginal Propensity to Consume} = \frac{\text{Change in Consumption}}{\text{Change in Income}}$$

$$MPC = \Delta C/\Delta Y$$

where Δ(delta) indicates the change (increase or decrease)

C = Consumption, Y = Income

Keynes said that the entire increased income cannot be spent on consumption only so some part of increased income will be saved by the community because (i) human wants are satiable and (ii) the application of law of diminishing marginal utility. So MPC is always less than one ($MPC<1$).

Like consumption, the savings is also related with the increase in income. "The ratio of change in savings to the change in income is called Marginal Propensity to Save." It can be expressed in the following formula:

$$\text{Marginal Propensity to Save} = \frac{\text{Change in Savings}}{\text{Change in Income}}$$

$$MPS = \Delta S/\Delta Y$$

The addition-sum of the change in consumption and change in savings is equal to the size of change in income so:

$$MPC + MPS = 1$$

Similarly,

$$MPC = 1 - MPS$$

or $$MPS = 1 - MPC$$

For example, if MPS is ¼, the value of MPC=1–MPS =1–¼ = ¾.

MPC and MPS can also be illustrated in Fig. 3.15

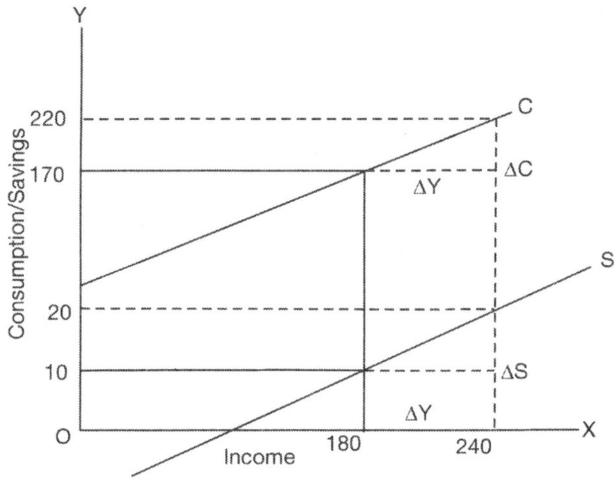

Fig. 3.15: MPC and MPS

In Fig. 3.15, C is consumption curve and S the savings curve.

ΔY = 240 – 180 = 60, ΔC = 220 – 170 = 50 and ΔS = 20 –10 = 10

Thus, by substituting these values in formulas:

MPC = ΔC/ΔY = 50/60 = 0.83

MPS = SΔ/ΔY = 10/60 = 0.17

Therefore,

MPC + MPS = 1 = 0.83 + 0.17

Thus the figure illustrates MPC and MPS.

In brief, APC, APS, MPC and MPS are also explained in Table 3.6.

Table 3.6: APC, APS, MPC and MPS

(₹ in Crore)

Income Y	Consumption C	APC =C/Y	APS =S/Y (1–APC)	MPC =ΔC/ΔY	MPS =ΔS/ΔY (1–MPC)
120	120	120/120 = 1	0	—	—
180	170	170/180 = 0.92	0.08	50/60=0.83	0.17
240	220	220/240 = 0.91	0.09	50/60=0.83	0.17
300	270	270/300 = 0.90	0.10	50/60=0.83	0.17
360	320	320/360 = 0.88	0.12	50/60=0.83	0.17

In case of linear consumption function, the value of MPC and MPS will remain constant.

The value of MPC determines the value of income multiplier so it plays crucial role in income generation. It remains constant in short-run as its determinants remain unchanged.

3.2.5 Determinants of Consumption Function

According to Keynes, there are two types of factors which influence the consumption function. They are (i) the subjective factors and (ii) the objective factors.

The subjective factors are endogenous or internal to the economic system. They include psychological characteristics of human nature and social practices, institutions and arrangements. They are unlikely to undergo a material change over a short period of time except in abnormal or revolutionary circumstances. They determine the slope and position of the consumption curve.

The objective factors are exogenous or external to the economic system. They may, therefore, undergo rapid changes and may cause marked shifts in consumption function.

(i) *Subjective Factors*

Keynes mentioned the following eight subjective factors which determine the level of consumption.

(a) **Individuals Motives:** There are eight motives which refrain individuals from spending their incomes entirely on consumption. They are (i) the desire to build reserves for unforeseen contingencies; (ii) the desire to provide for anticipated further needs, i.e. old age, sickness, etc.; (iii) the desire to enjoy an enlarged further income by way of interest and appreciation; (iv) the desire to enjoy a gradually increasing expenditure in order to improve the standard of living; (v) the desire to enjoy a sense of independence and power to do things; (vi) the desire to secure money to carry out speculative or business projects; (vii) the desire to bequeath a fortune; and (viii) the desire to satisfy a pure miserly instinct.

(b) **Business Motives:** The subjective factors are also influenced by the behavior of business corporations and governments. Keynes lists four motives for accumulation on their part: (i) enterprise—desire to do big things and to expand; (ii) liquidity—desire to meet emergencies and difficulties successfully; (iii) income raising—desire to save large income for successful management; and (iv) financial prudence—desire to provide adequate financial resources against depreciation and obsolescence and to discharge debt.

These factors remain constant during the short-run and keep the consumption function stable.

(ii) *Objective Factors*

Keynes suggested six objective factors which influence on consumption function. Modern economists like Prof. Dusenburry, Milton Friedman and others too suggested several other objective factors which influence on consumption function. They are as follow:

(a) **Changes in Wage Level:** If the wage rate rises, the consumption function shifts upwards. The workers having a high propensity to consume spend more out of their increased income and this tends to shift the consumption curve upward. If the rise in wage rate is accompanied by a more than proportionate rise in the price level, the real wage rate will fall and it will tend to shift the consumption curve downward.

(b) **Windfall Gains or Losses:** The unexpected changes in the stock market may lead either to gains or losses that tend to shift the consumption function upward or downward.

(c) **Changes in the Fiscal Policy:** The changes in the fiscal policy of the government in the form of taxation and public expenditure affect the aggregate consumption function. Heavy commodity taxation adversely affects the consumption by reducing the disposable income of the people. On the other hand, the policy of progressive taxation along with that of public expenditure on welfare programme tends to shift the consumption function upward by altering the distribution of income.

(d) **Changes in Expectations:** The changes in expectation regarding price in future also affect consumption. If a rise in price expected in near future, the people buy much in excess of their current needs and consumption function shifts upward. If prices are likely to fall in future, people will buy only necessary things and this will lead to fall in consumption demand and total consumption curve falls downward.

(e) **Changes in the Rate of Interest:** Substantial changes in the market rate of interest may influence the consumption function indirectly. A rise in the rate of interest will encourage people to spend less on consumption in order to avail the opportunity.

(f) **Financial Policies of Corporations:** The financial policies of corporations with regard to income retention, dividend payments and reinvestment tend to affect the consumption function in several ways. If the corporation keeps more profit in the form of reserves, dividend payments to shareholders will be less.

It reduces the income of the shareholders and thus the consumption level.

(g) **Holding of Liquid Assets:** The amount of liquid assets in the form of cash balances, savings and government bonds in the hands of consumers also influence the consumption function. If people hold larger liquid assets they will have a tendency to spend less income on consumption.

(h) **Distribution of Income:** The pattern of distribution of income in a community also determines the consumption function. If there are large disparities in the income distribution between the rich and poor, the consumption function will be low because the rich have a law propensity to consume and the poor with a very law income and unable spend to more on consumption. Thus, the high MPC of the poor remains unsatisfied. The redistribution of income depends on the government economic policies.

(i) **Attitude towards Saving:** The aggregate consumption function is also influenced by people's attitude towards saving. If they value future consumption is more than present consumption they will tend to save more and consumption function will shift downward.

(j) **Demonstration Effect:** According to Prof. Dusenburry, the consumption standard of the low-income group-people is always influenced by the consumption standard of high income group-people. The moment low-income group-people start consuming goods used by high income groups, the latter always try to avoid consumption of such commodities and search for still further better commodities. Such tendencies go to increase consumption and weakness the propensity to save. Thus, it influence on consumption level which is called 'Dusenburry Hypothesis'.

(k) **Changes in Consumer's Tastes and Fashions:** Changes in consumers' tastes and fashions may also affect the propensity to consume, although such changes shall not be substantial enough to affect it in the short-run.

(l) **Consumer Credit:** The availability of consumer credit places extra purchasing power in the hands of the individuals to buy consumer goods over and above those which he could purchase with his regular income. Facilities of buying on installment basis have been instrumental in raising consumption function in Western countries.

(m) **Permanent Income Hypothesis:** Milton Friedman argues that the permanent consumption depends on permanent income and temporary consumption on temporary consumption. So the change in any type of income leads to change in consumption.

3.2.6 Importance of Consumption Function

Keynes consumption function is an outstanding contribution to economic analysis. Prof. A.H. Hanson called it a milestone in the history of economic literature. The following points suggest the importance of consumption function in modern economic theory.

(i) Crucial Importance of Investment: Keynes' Psychological Law of Consumption stresses on the vital point that people fail to spend their entire increased income on consumption. This tendency creates a gap between income and consumption which can only be filled by either investment or consumption. If either of them fails to the gap, the output and employment will inevitably fall in the economy. Since the consumption function is stable in the short-run, the gap between income and consumption can only be filled by an increase in investment. Thus, the psychological law emphasizes the crucial role of investment in Keynes' theory. It is inadequacy of investment which results unemployment and thus investment should be increased to overcome unemployment problem.

(ii) Condemns Say's Law: Say's law states that supply always creates its own demand so there is equality between demand and supply, income and expenditure and savings and investment. Therefore, there cannot be general overproduction or general unemployment. But Keynes's psychological law does not agree the Say's law because the entire increase in income may not be spent on consumption so there need not be equality between income and expenditure, demand and supply and savings and investment. Thus, supply fails to create its own demand. Rather it exceeds demand and leads to general overproduction and glut of commodities in the market.

(iii) Declining Tendency of the Marginal Efficiency of Capital: The psychological law also points out that since MPC is less than one, there is tendency of declining marginal efficiency of capital in a laissez-fair economy. This results in deficiency of demand in the market. The producers will reduce production which will in turn bring a decline in the demand for capital goods, expected rate of profit and business expectations. It implies a decline in the marginal efficiency of capital. It is not possible to arrest this process of declining tendency of marginal efficiency of capital unless there is rise in propensity to consume.

(iv) Secular Stagnation: According to A.H. Hanson, the under-consumption or MPC<1 would generally result into stagnation in long-run which is called 'Secular Stagnation'. Prof. R.G. Lipsey defines it as "conditions of chronic excess of desired savings over desired private investment have been called conditions of secular stagnation". Thus, the consumption function theory helps us to explain the phenomenon of secular stagnation.

(v) State Intervention: The consumption function theory reputes the classicals belief of automatic adjustment in the economy in long-run. The theory suggests state intervention to control economic activities during inflation or deflation.

(vi) Turning Points of Business Cycle: Consumption function helps to explain the turning points of the business cycle. The economy swings down from the peak because marginal propensity to consume is less than one. Likewise, economy's downward movement stops and it starts recovery because marginal propensity to consume being less than one, people do not reduce their consumption as much as the reduction in their income. Even during depression people try to maintain their previous level of consumption.

(vii) Role in Income Generation: In income multiplier theory, the process of income generation in the economy depends upon the value income multiplier, i.e. k. In fact, the value of multiplier is derived from the value of marginal propensity to consume, i.e. Multiplier (k) = 1 /1–MPC: higher the MPC, the higher the value of multiplier and lower the MPC, lower will be the value of k.

3.3 INVESTMENT FUNCTION

Investment plays an important role in income and employment determination. Investment refers to the demand for capital goods so it is a part of aggregate demand which determines the level of income and employment in the economy.

3.3.1 Meaning

Keynes defines investment as "net addition to real capital". In other words, investment means real investment, i.e. purchasing of new building, new machines and construction of new factory buildings, roads, bridges and other forms of productive capital stock of the community, including increase in inventories. It does not include the purchase of old or existing stocks, shares, buildings, machines, securities and others which constitute merely an exchange of money from one person to another. Such investment is merely financial investment and does not affect the level of employment in an economy. It is only real investment which gives additional employment to the people. According to Stonier and Hague, "By investment, we do not mean the purchase of existing paper securities, bonds, debentures or equities but the purchase of new factories, machines and the like". Mrs. Joan Robinson defines it as "investment means an addition to the stock of goods in existence".

3.3.2 Types of Investment

There are various types of investments. Generally, they are classified as under:

(i) **Gross Investment and Net Investment:** Gross investment refers to the total investment including replacement investment. Using of new capital goods in place of old and worn-out capital goods is called "replacement investment". It can be written as: GI=NI+RI,

where GI=Gross Investment, NI=Net Investment, RI = Replacement Investment.

Net investment is the gross investment minus replacement investment. It means net addition to capital stock. It is written as: NI=GI–RI.

Net investment plays important role in generation of income and employment in the economy.

(ii) **Ex-ante and Ex-post Investment:** Ex-ante investment refers to planned or anticipated or intended investment. Ex-post investment refers to actually realized investment. The ex-ante investment influences on economic activities and may cause fluctuations in them.

(iii) **Private Investment and Public Investment:** Investment by private individuals or organizations is called private investment and public investment is by the government.

Private investment is influenced by marginal efficiency of capital (i.e. profit expectations) and the rate of interest. It is profit elastic.

Public investment is undertaken by the state or local authorities such as building of roads, irrigation projects, school buildings, public parks, electricity works, etc. Public investment does not consider profit motive. It is undertaken for social good and not for private gain.

(iv) Autonomous Investment and Induced Investment: Autonomous investment and induced investment play important role in the theory of income and employment.

Autonomous investment is that investment which is independent of the rate of interest and marginal efficiency of capital (MEC) or rate of return (both are forms of income). It depends upon the government budgetary policy and public requirements. Autonomous investment takes the form of houses, roads, public undertakings and infrastructural facilities like generation of power, transport and communication. Investment made by the government. It is dependent on factors like growth in population and progress in technology, etc. The objective of autonomous investment is to accelerate development in the economy.

Autonomous investment can be represented in Fig. 3.16 below:

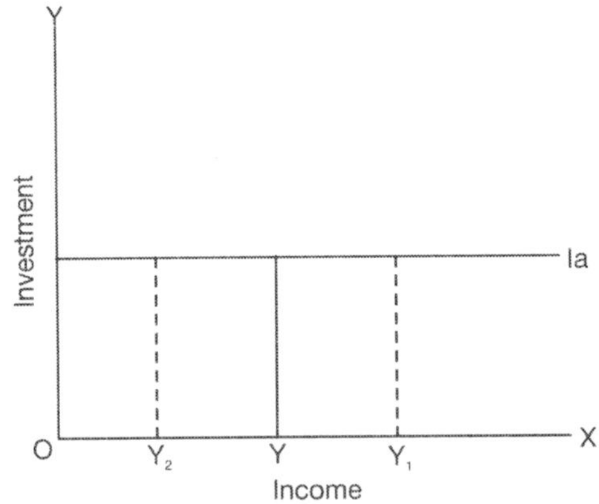

Fig. 3.16: Autonomous Investment

Investment is shown along OY axis and income is measured along the OX axis. Ia is the investment curve drawn parallel to the OX axis. This means that the level of investment same at the different level of income, i.e. Y, Y_1 and Y_2.

The investment which is induced by change in income, i.e. MEC and rate of interest is called induced investment. Induced investment is illustrated in Fig. 3.17.

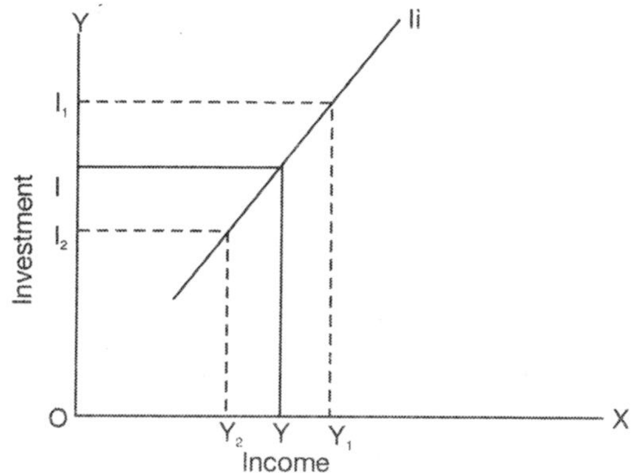

Fig. 3.17: Induced Investment

As before, income is shown along OX and investment along OY. The investment curve Ii has been shown as easing upward to the right. This means that as income increases from Y to Y_1, investment also increases from I to I_1, and as income decreases from Y to Y_2 investment too decreases I_2. Induced investment is income-elastic so it is written as:

$$Ii = f(Y)$$

where Ii = Induced Investment, f = functional relation and Y = Income.

3.3.3 Keynes' Investment Function

Investment function refers the functional relation between investment and rate of interest and marginal efficiency of capital. Classical economists consider investment is oppositely related with the interest rate. So expressed the investment function as:

$$I= f(r)$$

where I = investment, r = rate of interest and f = functional relation.

But according to Keynes investment function refers to the functional relational between rate of interest and marginal efficiency of capital. He expresses it as:

$$I= f(r, MEC)$$

where I = investment, r = rate of interest f = functional relation and MEC = marginal efficiency of capital.

Keynes' investment function can be shown in Fig. 3.18

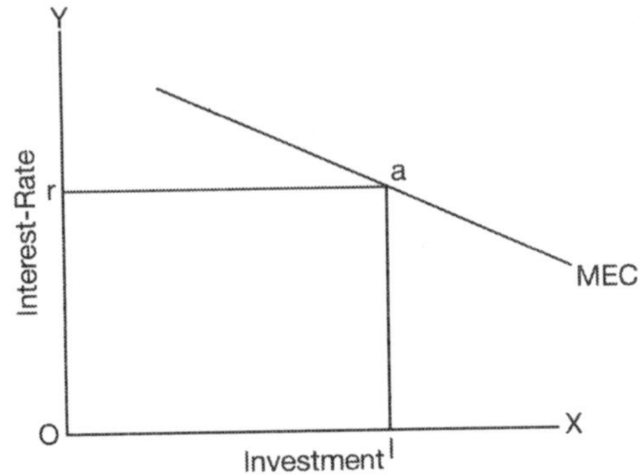

Fig. 3.18: Investment Function

MEC curve represents marginal efficiency of capital. Rate of interest is measured along OY axis and the investment along OX axis. There is inverse relation between r and MEC. When the rate of interest is r, the MEC is a so the level of investment is I.

Keynes further argues that since there is no change in interest rate policy of central and commercial banks, the rate of interest remains constant in short-run. Hence, the investment depends on MEC in short-run. He writes it as:

$$I = f(MEC)$$

3.3.4 Determinants of Investment

According to Keynes, rate of interest and marginal efficiency of capital are the two factors which determine the investment. They are shown as under:

(i) *Rate of Interest (R)*

According to Keynes, interest is the reward or price to be for parting with liquidity. When a person is giving money or a part of his income to another person, he is parting with purchasing power for a given period so he must be paid some reward for it. Liquidity generally means the purchasing or converting power over goods and services.

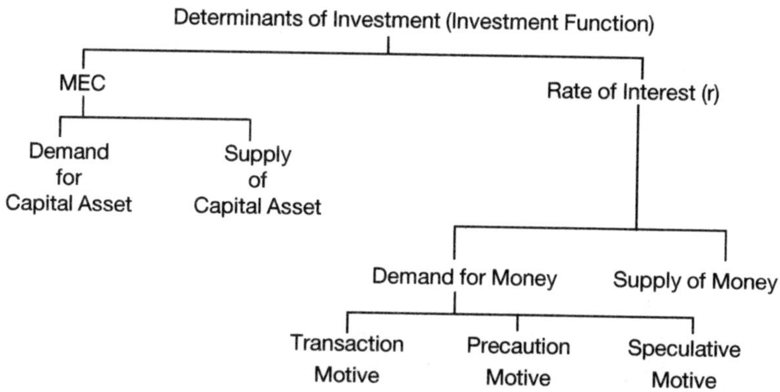

Keynes has propounded a separate theory on rate of interest determination which is popularly known as 'Liquidity Preference Theory on Interest'. The theory said that in money market the demand for money or cash balance and the supply of money determine the rate of interest. In other words, the equilibrium between demand for and supply of money determines rate of interest in the economy. At a given supply of money, greater the liquidity preference, the greater will be the rate of interest. Given the liquidity preference and the income level greater the supply of money, the lower will be the rate of interest. So changes in demand and supply of money will change rate of interest in the economy.

But according to Keynes, since the central and commercial bank policies remain unchanged, the rate of interest remains constant in short-run. Hence, the marginal efficiency of capital plays vital role in determination of income and employment in the economy in short-run.

(ii) *Marginal Efficiency of Capital (MEC)*

Marginal efficiency of capital is the determinant of investment in particular and income and employment in general.

MEC means the expected rate of return or profit of a new additional capital unit over its cost. In other words, it is the expected income or yield from the additional unit of capital employed in business or industry. Machines, inventories, assets, etc. are the examples of capital goods or assets.

Businessmen always compare MEC with supply price of capital asset while undertaking investment. The supply price of capital asset means the replacement cost of that asset when it would wear out. Every capital asset has its life span and during its life span it yields income which is called 'Perspective Yield' or 'Rate of Return'. Further Keynes argues that since the value of money declines in future or increases in price of the capital asset the perspective yields or future annuities or money income should be discounted at a particular rate in order to make it equal to the supply price of capital asset in future. He said that the present value of the prospective yield depends upon the rate of discount and MEC is just equal to the rate of discount.

Hence, Keynes defines MEC as "MEC as being equal to the rate of discount which would make the present value of the series of annuities given by the returns expected from the capital asset during its life just equal to its supply price". Prof. Kurihar made it clearer by his definition as "It is the ratio between the perspective yield of additional capital goods and their supply price". So it can be found out as:

$$\text{MEC} = \text{Rate of Discount} = \frac{\text{Prospective Yield}}{\text{Supply Price of Capital}}$$

For example, the prospective yield of a capital asset is ₹ 1000 and its supply price is ₹ 10000 so the rate of discount is worked out as under:

$$\text{Rate of Discount} = \frac{1000}{10000} = 0.1 \text{ or in percentage} = 0.1 \times 100$$

$= 10\%$.

Determinants of MEC

MEC depends upon two factors, namely (i) supply price of capital asset and (ii) demand price of capital asset.

(i) **Supply Price of Capital Asset:** The discounted prospective yield of an asset is called 'Supply Price of Capital Asset'. It is also called 'Replacement Cost'. The capital asset yields income every year during its life-time so it should be discounted for finding out its supply price. It can be expressed in following formula as:

Supply Price of Capital Asset = Discounted Prospective Yields

$$Cr = \frac{Q_1}{(1+r)^1} + \frac{Q_2}{(1+r)^2} + \frac{Q_3}{(1+r)^3} + \ldots + \frac{Q_n}{(1+r)^n}$$

where Cr = supply price or replacement cost of new capital assets, Q_1, Q_2, Q_3,..., Q_n = expected annual returns from the capital asset (also referred to as the series of prospective annual yields), and r = rate of discount or MEC which will make the present value of annual returns just equal to supply price of capital asset.

For example, a sewing machine is a capital asset so its life span is three years and it yields income as Q_1 = ₹ 500, Q_2 = ₹ 1000 and Q_3 = 1500. The rate of discount is 10 per cent (0.1). The supply price of sewing machine can be worked out with help of above formula.

$$Cr = \frac{Q_1}{(1+r)^1} + \frac{Q_2}{(1+r)^2} + \frac{Q_3}{(1+r)^3}$$

By substituting the above values in the equation

$$\therefore \quad Cr = \frac{500}{(1+0.1)^1} + \frac{1000}{(1+0.1)^2} + \frac{1500}{(1+0.1)^3}$$

$$Cr = \frac{500}{1.1} + \frac{1000}{1.21} + \frac{1500}{1.331}$$

$$= 454.55 + 826.45 + 1126.97 = 2407.97$$

The above given example can also be illustrated as the supply price or replacement cost of a sewing machine is ₹ 2407.97 and its life is three years and expected return from it for the first year will be ₹ 500, the second year ₹ 1000 and the third year ₹ 1500. When the expected returns are discounted by 10 per cent discount rate the present value of the total returns will be ₹ 2407.97 which is just equal to the current supply price of the sewing machine.

(ii) Demand Price of Capital Asset: The investors use either their own fund or borrowed fund. However, the interest rate has to be taken into consideration. The demand price of capital asset can be calculated on the basis of rate of interest.

Keynes defined demand price of a capital asset as "the sum of the expected future yields discounted at the current rate of interest". It can be written as:

Demand Price = Sum of the prospective yields discounted at the current rate of interest.

$$K = \frac{Q_1}{(1+i)^1} + \frac{Q_2}{(1+i)^2} + \frac{Q_3}{(1+i)^3} + \ldots + \frac{Q_n}{(1+i)^n}$$

where v = demand price, Q_1, Q_2, Q_3,..., Q_n, prospective yield or annuities and i = current rate of interest.

In brief, the demand price of capital asset is the present value of capital asset. By continuing the above example, the demand price of sewing machine can be calculated with the help of its above equation. Rate of interest 5 per cent is taken in place of discount rate because assuming that the money is borrowed from bank for purchasing of sewing machine.

$$V = \frac{Q_1}{(1+i)^1} + \frac{Q_2}{(1+i)^2} + \frac{Q_3}{(1+i)^3}$$

By substituting the above values in the equation

$$V = \frac{500}{(1+0.05)^1} + \frac{1000}{(1+.05)^2} + \frac{1500}{(1+.05)^3}$$

$$= \frac{500}{1.05} + \frac{1000}{1.10} + \frac{1500}{1.16}$$

$$= 476.19 + 909.91 + 1293.10 = 2679.20$$

The demand price of capital asset depends on the current rate of interest: lower the rate of interest, higher will be the demand price; higher the current rate of interest, lower will be the demand price of capital asset. The investor always thinks of rate of interest: even if he invests his own fund because it will earn interest if deposits in the bank or lends loan to others. Further the investor compares between demand price and supply of capital asset. If the demand price of capital asset is greater than supply price of capital asset, more investment will take place. On contrary, it is vice versa.

3.3.5 Relation between Investment, Rate of Interest and MEC

There is inverse relation between investment and marginal efficiency of capital. Whenever there is increase in investment MEC declines because of the reasons (i) as investment increases the demand for capital goods also increases but due to inelastic supply of capital goods only their price increases much and (ii) increase in investment results into increase in production of consumers' good so their price declines much. On the contrary, whenever investment declines, the MEC will go-up because of reverse working of the said reasons. Rate of interest also influence on MEC thereby on investment. These relations are explained in Table 3.7.

Table 3.7: Relation between Investment and MEC

MEC (r)	Rate of Interest (i)	Investment
10%	8%	Increases
8%	8%	Neutral
6%	8%	Decreases

If MEC is greater than rate of interest, the investment will increase or if MEC is equal to rate of interest, there will no change in investment or if rate of interest is higher than MEC, the investment will decrease. MEC is also known as 'Investment Demand' (ID). The relation between MEC, interest rate and investment are illustrated in Fig. 3.19.

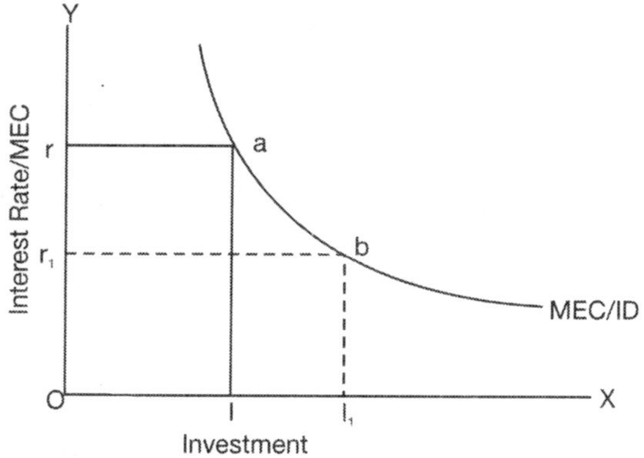

Fig. 3.19: Relation between MEC, Interest Rate and Investment

Investment is measured along OX axis and MEC/rate of interest is measured along OY axis. The MEC/ID curve represents the marginal efficiency of capital or investment demand. At r rate of interest, MEC is at a and the investment is OI. When rate of interest declines to r_1, MEC moves to b so the investment will increase to I_1. Hence, there is inverse relation between MEC/rate of interest and investment.

The volume of investment depends upon the shape of MEC or ID curve but the shape of ID curve depends upon whether investment is interest elastic or inelastic. These relations are illustrated in Fig. 3.20

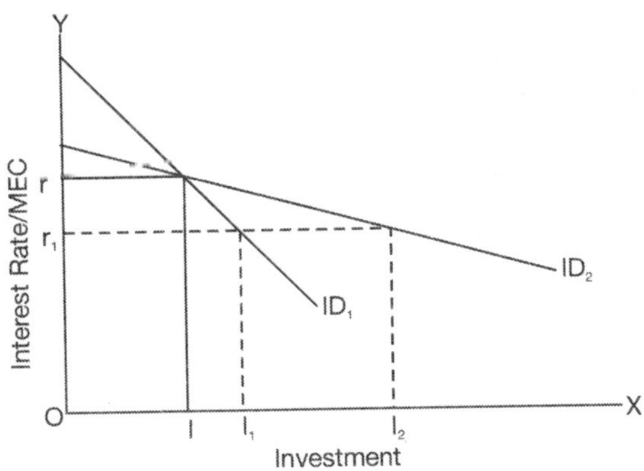

Fig. 3.20: Relation between MEC Interest Rate and Investment

ID_1 curve represents the interest inelastic investment demand and it means a greater change in rate of interest leads a smaller change in investment. When interest rate declines to r_1, the investment will increase to I_1 which is less than change in interest rate.

ID_2 curve represents the interest elastic investment demand and it means a smaller change in rate of interest leads a greater change in investment. When interest rate declines to r_1, the investment will increase to I_2 which is greater than change in interest rate.

On the other hand, if the investment is perfectly interest elastic, the change in investment will be infinity so the ID curve will be horizontal and parallel to OX axis. It is shown in Fig. 3.21.

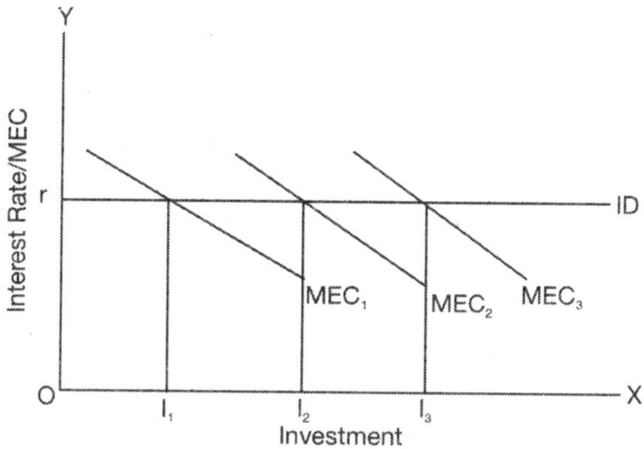

Diagram 3.21: Relation between MEC Interest Rate and Investment

ID curve shows that a little change in interest rate leads to innumerous or infinite change in investment.

In brief, however, Keynes argues that the change in business expectations will influence on investment through MEC in short-run where the interest rate is constant.

3.3.6 Factors Influencing the Marginal Efficiency of Capital (MEC)

There are a large number of factors which influence the marginal efficiency of capital in an economy. On the basis of time element, they are classified and studied as under:

(A) *Short-Run-Factors*

The following are the short-run-factors which influence the marginal efficiency of capital.

(i) **Nature of Demand, Cost and Prices:** MEC depends upon the nature of demand. If demand is more sensitive to the expectation of future changes in income, cost and price, the MEC will be more variable. If incomes are expected to increase in future, consumption tends to rise which leads to rise in expected demand so also MEC rises due to rise in price of consumers goods. Similarly, if the costs and prices increase, the MEC will decline. On the contrary, it is vice versa.

(ii) **Propensity to Consume:** The change in level of consumption would also influence MEC through the change in investment. For instance, if the level of consumption per unit of income increases, more investment will take place to increase the production of consumer goods which will raise the demand for capital goods that will decline MEC due to rise in price of capital goods.

(iii) Changes in Income: The windfall profits or losses, tax concession or levies, etc. bring sudden changes in income which influences the marginal efficiency of capital. For example, a sudden rise in profits due to increase in demand or tax relaxation will raise the MEC.

(iv) Change in Liquidity Assets: MEC depends upon the liquidity nature of asset. If the asset is more liquidity in nature, the investment will increase that will reduce the MEC.

(v) Waves of Optimism and Pessimism: Psychological factors play an important role in determining the MEC. If the businessmen are optimistic regarding the business in future, more investment will take place thereby the MEC will decline. On the contrary, it will be vice versa.

(B) *Long-Run Factors*

Like short-run factors, the long-run factors to influence the MEC. They are discussed as under:

(i) Population Growth: The size and growth rate of population would influence the MEC through the size of investment. A fast growing population invariably raises the demand for consumer goods initially which raises MEC but later when more investments take place to meet the growing demand of the consumers, the MEC decline will decline due to rise in price of capital goods in future.

(ii) Technique of Production: MEC depends upon the technique or method of production. An improvement in technology or methods of production saves costs of all types which will raise the MEC. The primitive or outdated techniques always add more costs thus MEC will be low.

(iii) Supply of Capital Goods: The level of investment whether increases or decreases in the economy, but its effect on MEC will depend upon the nature of supply of capital goods like machineries, equipments, etc. If supply of capital goods is more elastic, the increase in investment will not reduce the MEC.

3.3.7 MEC and Expectations

According to Keynes, MEC depends upon the supply-price and demand-price of capital assets or capital goods. The prospective yield of any capital asset or investment generally depends on two things, namely (i) existing or current events and (ii) future factors.

Keynes further argued that the existing events which are more or less ascertained and future factors cannot be anticipated with confidence. The investment decisions are governed by expectations of yields but not by actual yields. The purchase of durable capital assets requires huge immediate expenditures before any actual returns begins to flow back to the entrepreneur. Thus, capital assets are a link between the present and the uncertain future. It is, therefore, essential to analyze the true nature of business expectations and their influence on MEC.

According to Keynes, there are two types of business expectations, (i) short-run expectations, (ii) long-run expectations.

(i) Short-run Expectations: Short-run expectations are related to the sale of output from the existing plants. In short-run, the plants are fixed or unchangeable but only the output is variable as it concern to the current events which arise from events in the recent past. Short-run expectations are based upon the factors such as the price and wage levels, employment, interest rates, money supply, etc. operating in the recent past. In comparison with the long-run expectations, the short-run expectations are more stable because the events in the short-period tend themselves to definite conclusions whereas events in the distant future cannot form the basis of definite and settled conclusions. Furthermore, the short-run expectations are more continuous than the long-run expectations because there is greater degree of continuity over the short-period than over the long-period. Since short-run expectations are more stable and continuous, they cannot adequately explain the fluctuations in the volume of investment.

(ii) Long-run Expectations: Long-run expectations are the real determinants of the MEC. Long-run expectations are concerned with future events which cannot be forecasted with confidence. Events such as outbreak of war, possibility of peace, changes in technology, and the size and compositions of population will the long-run expectations.

Long-run expectations relate to the variations in the sale of output in the long-run that depends upon the changes in scale of production and the size of existing plants and new plants. So the long-run expectations regarding prospective yields of new capital assets are very unstable and uncertain. Since the long-run expectations regarding the prospective yields of capital assets are uncertain, there are more variations in MEC so Keynes said that there are more fluctuations in the induced investment. Further he suggested that there is need for socialization of investment in the economy for attaining stability.

3.4 INVESTMENT MULTIPLIER THEORY

3.4.1 The Concept of Multiplier

The concept of multiplier was first developed by Prof. R.F. Kahn in his article, "The Relation of Home Investment to Unemployment" in 1931. Kahn's Multiplier was the 'Employment Multiplier'. He explained that the generation of total employment in the economy depends on the size of employment generation in the primary occupations like public works activities such as constructions of public buildings, roads, bridges, etc. which are called primary employment. For instance, if a road is undertaken for construction by the primary investment, some laborers would be employed directly but it also leads to demand for construction-materials so for producing them more laborers would be employed in secondary occupations which eventually generates more total employment in the economy. Prof. Kahn explained his 'Employment Multiplier' as:

$$K = \frac{N_2}{N_1}$$

where K = Employment Multiplier, N_1 = Primary Employment, N_2 = Total Employment.

$$\therefore N_2 = K \times N_1$$

Keynes used the multiplier concept to explain the relation between changes in investment to change in income propagation. Keynes concept of multiplier is more popular as 'Investment Multiplier' or 'Income Multiplier'. It is an integral part of his theory of income and employment. It is Keynes' path-breaking contribution to economic analysis. Economists before Keynes were aware of the relation of an increment of investment to an increment of income but they did not express this in a precise and well-defined form. Hence, development of this concept credit goes to Keynes.

3.4.2 Meaning and Definition

Keynes said in his investment multiplier theory that the change in autonomous investment would result into the change in income, consumption, savings, investment, etc. in the economy. He suggested it as a tool to avoid economic depression. His Investment Multiplier expresses the relationship between an initial increment in investment and the final increment in aggregate income. According to Keynes' income multiplier, when investment increases, as a result of it the income will increase by k time, i.e. the value of multiplier. Thus, Keynes defines investment multiplier as "the ratio of the change in income to the change in investment". Prof. A.H. Hansen defines Keynes' investment multiplier as "the coefficient relating to an increment of investment to an increment of income". It shows how many times the aggregate income would increase as a result of increase in investment. So Keynes expresses his investment multiplier in equation-form as:

$$Y = kI$$

$$\therefore \Delta Y = kI$$

where Y = Income, I = Investment, k = Multiplier and = Δ change.

For example, if the value of k = 4 and I = ₹ 200 crore, then the value of change in income, i.e.

$$\Delta Y = k\Delta I$$

$$= 4 \times ₹\ 200 \text{ crore} = ₹\ 800 \text{ crore}$$

The change in income is four times greater than increase in investment. The number of times income increases due to increase in investment through marginal propensity to consume (MPC) is called 'Multiplier Effect'.

Further Keynes argues that the value of multiplier, i.e. k basically depends upon the value of marginal propensity to consume (MPC). So he expressed the value of k as:

$$k = \frac{1}{1 - MDC}$$

where k = Multiplier and MPC = Marginal Propensity to Consume, i.e. $\frac{\Delta c}{\Delta y}$. So it can be written as:

$$k = \frac{1}{1 - \frac{\Delta c}{\Delta y}}$$

It is also learnt that the sum of marginal propensity to consume and marginal propensity to save is always equal to one, i.e. MPC + MPS = 1 or $\frac{\Delta C}{\Delta Y} + \frac{\Delta S}{\Delta Y} = 1$. Therefore, the value of multiplier can also be written as:

$$K = \frac{1}{1 - \frac{\Delta C}{\Delta Y}} = \frac{1}{1 - MPC} = \frac{1}{MPS}, \text{ since MPS = 1 – MPC.}$$

Hence, the value of multiplier depends upon the value of MPC or MPS.

3.4.3 Relation between MPC and k

Since the initial increment of investment produces multiple effects on the final increase in income through changes in consumption expenditure, the value of multiplier is determined by the marginal propensity to consume or MPC. There is a direct or positive relationship between MPC and k.

Higher the marginal propensity to consume, higher will be the value of multiplier; lower the marginal propensity to consume, lower will be the value of the multiplier. In fact, the size of the multiplier is derived from MPC or MPS. The relationship between the multiplier and marginal propensity to consume is derived from the income-equation. It is explained as under:

$$Y = C + S$$
$$\Delta Y = \Delta C + \Delta S$$

Since increased income is distributed as expenditure on consumption and savings, it can be written as:

$$\frac{\Delta C}{\Delta Y} + \frac{\Delta S}{\Delta Y} = \frac{\Delta Y}{\Delta Y} = 1$$

or it can also be written as:

$$MPC + MPS = 1$$

For example, if $\Delta Y = 100$, $\Delta C = 75$ and $\Delta S = 25$, by substituting these values in the above equations the statement can be verified as:

$$100 = 75 + 25$$
$$\therefore \quad \frac{75}{100} + \frac{25}{100} = \frac{100}{100} = 1$$

Here

$$MPC = \frac{75}{100} = 0.75 \text{ and}$$
$$MPS = \frac{25}{100} = 0.25$$
$$\therefore \quad 0.75 + 0.25 = 1$$

The value of multiplier (k) depends upon the value of MPC or MPS. So it is written as:

$K = \frac{1}{1 - \frac{\Delta C}{\Delta Y}} = \frac{1}{1 - MPC} = \frac{1}{MPS}$. Thus, k is the reciprocal of MPS, i.e. MPS = 0.25 or $\frac{1}{4}$

so $K = \frac{1}{\frac{2}{4}} = 4$

The value of k can be derived from the original multiplier equation as:

$$k\Delta I = \Delta Y$$

$\therefore K = \frac{\Delta Y}{\Delta I}$ since $\Delta Y = \Delta C + \Delta I$ (Expenditure Equation), $\Delta I = \Delta Y - \Delta C$

By substituting the value of I in the k value equation, we get:

$$k = \frac{\Delta Y}{\Delta I} = \frac{\Delta Y}{\Delta Y - \Delta C}$$

Further dividing numerator and denominator by Y, we get:

$$k = \frac{\Delta Y / \Delta Y}{\Delta Y / \Delta Y - \Delta C / \Delta Y} = \frac{1}{1 - \Delta C / \Delta Y} = \frac{1}{1 - MPC} = \frac{1}{MPS}$$

Thus, we get the value of k.

From this it is clear that value of k depends upon the value of MPC.

The value of k corresponding to the value of MPC is shown in Table 3.8 provided we know the marginal propensity to consume or marginal propensity to save. The relationship between MPC, MPS and k can be shown in Table 3.8.

Table 3.8: Value of k corresponding to the value of MPC

MPC	MPS	k
0	1	1
1/2	1/2	2
2/3	1/3	3
1/4	1/4	4
4/5	1/5	5
8/9	1/9	9
9/10	1/10	10
1	0	∞ (infinity)

The above table shows that the value of the multiplier varies directly with MPC and inversely with MPS.

Keynes said that the value of MPC lies between greater than zero and less than one, i.e. MPC > 0 but < 1. So the value of MPC never fall to zero, therefore the value of k cannot be equal to one. Since MPC is always less than one (MPC < 1), the value of k cannot infinity (∞).

3.4.4 Assumptions

The multiplier theory is also based on certain assumptions. It will operate fully well only if these assumptions are actually realized in practice. Therefore, in a strict sense, these assumptions also act as limitations on the working of multiplier.

(i) **Availability of Consumer Goods:** The process of income generation through multiplier is subject to the availability of consumer goods. If the consumer goods are available in adequate quantity, the multiplier will continue to work.

(ii) **Increase in Investment should be Prolonged:** The new level of investment should be prolonged till the completion of the multiplier process. In other words, it is necessary that the increments in investment be repeated at regular intervals for successful working of multiplier process. In case it is not done so the income cannot rise. If there is a break in the continuity of investments, national income will rapidly fall back to its original level. Thus, a continuing stream of new investment is indispensable for the working of multiplier.

(iii) **Net Increase in Investment:** For successful working of multiplier, there should be a net increase in investment in the economy. In other words, an act of investment in one sector should not be offset by an act of disinvestments in some other sector of the economy. Otherwise, it will affect adversely on the working of multiplier.

(iv) **There should not be Induced Investment:** The multiplier theory has assumed only the autonomous investment. It has not taken induced investment because it depends upon interest-rate and marginal efficiency of capital. The variations in them obstruct the working of multiplier.

(v) **No Change in MPC:** The multiplier theory has assumed that there should be no change in the value of marginal propensity to consume during the process. The multiplier coefficient depends upon MPC so any change in value of MPC will affect adversely on the working of multiplier.

(vi) **Existence of Closed Economy:** It also assumed the closed economy that is the country has no trade relations with the outside world. If the country has trade relations with other countries, the export and import trade will affect adversely on the working of multiplier. Suppose the country has export surplus, there will be a net addition to the income stream, as the other countries pay for excess imports and the value of the multiplier may become greater than its anticipated value. On the contrary, if there is import surplus, there will be leakage from the income stream and the value of the multiplier may turn out to be less than its anticipated value.

(vii) No Time Lags between Successive Expenditure on Consumption: It is assumed that there are no time lags in the multiplier process. To achieve the full value of the multiplier, there should not be any time intervals between the receipt of the income and spending of it. In other words, consumers should spend the income as soon as they receive it. An increase (decrease) in investment instantaneously leads to a multiple increase (decrease) in income.

(viii) Existence of Less than Full Employment: The multiplier theory assumes the existence of involuntary unemployment in the economy. So long as there is unemployed resources and idle capacity, income, output and employment will continue to expand on account of the operation of the multiplier. So it assumed the existence of less than full employment.

(ix) Easy Availability of Other Resources: It is also assumed that other resources of production are also easily available within the country.

(x) Price Stability: It assumes internal price stability for the working of multiplier.

3.4.5 Working of Investment Multiplier

The multiplier theory explains the cumulative effect of a change in autonomous investment on income through its effect on consumption. An increase in investment leads to an increased production which creates income and generates consumption expenditure. This process continues in dwindling series till no further increase in income and expenditure is possible. The working of multiplier is explained with single and prolonged expenditure on autonomous investment.

(i) Investment Multiplier with Single Expenditure on Investment: The process of income generation through multiplier can be illustrated by means of an arithmetical example. It also explains multiplier effect on income with a single expenditure made on investment. Keynes has used simultaneous or no time-lag process in a static framework explain the working of investment multiplier.

For example, in an economy MPC is ½ and ₹ 100 crore is the autonomous investment made on public works. This will immediately generate income by ₹ 100 crore. Since the value of MPC is ½ or 0.5, half of this new income will be spent immediately on consumption goods which will lead to increase in production and income by the same amount and so on. The whole process is explained in Table 3.9.

Table 3.9: Example Showing Working of Multiplier

Period	Increment in investment ΔI (in crore)	Increment in income Y	$\Delta C = C\Delta Y$ MPC = 0.5	$S = (\Delta Y - \Delta C)$ increment in saving
0	-	-	-	-
1	100 →	100	50	50
		50	25	25
		25	12.5	12.50
		12.5	6.25	6.25
		6.250	3.12	3.12
		So on...	...	...
Final	100	200	100	100

The table reveals that an increment of ₹ 100 crore of investment in the primary round leads to the same increase in income. Of this one half or ₹ 50 crore are saved and ₹ 50 crore are spent on consumption which will generate income by the same amount in the second round. This process of income generation continues in the secondary round and till the total income generated rises to ₹ 200 crore. The initial investment of ₹ 100 crore creates ₹ 50 crore, 25 crore, 12.5 crore, 6.25 crore, 3.12 crore and so on till the further division of income becomes impossible. By adding up all these incomes generated, the total generated income will go up to ₹ 200 crore which is two times the original investment. According to Keynes, this whole process is completed without any time-lag or time-gap.

The working of the multiplier can also be explained with the help of Fig. 3.22.

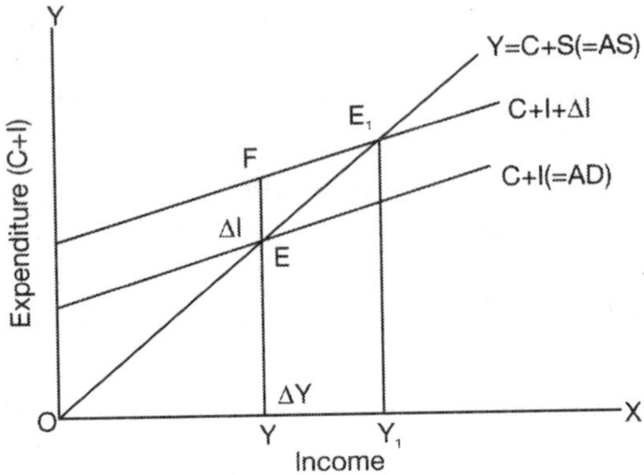

Fig. 3.22: Working of Multiplier

The expenditure (consumption + investment) is measured along OX axis and the income along OY axis. Y=C+S (aggregate supply) is money income supply curve and C+I is aggregate demand curve. Both AS and AD curves are intersected each other at E so the equilibrium income is Y. Now a new autonomous investment has taken place, i.e. EF (ΔI) as a result of it through multiplier effect the equilibrium moves from E to E_1 and the income increases to Y_1.

Backward or Reverse Working of the Multiplier

So far, we have studied the forward working of the multiplier due to increase in investment. On the contrary, if the investment decreases, the multiplier operates backwards or it produces reverse effect.

A reduction in investment will lead to contraction of income and consumption, which in turn will lead to cumulative decline in income, and consumption till the contraction in aggregate income is the multiple of the initial decrease in investment suppose investment decreases by ₹ 100 crore. With MPC = 0.5 and k =2, consumption expenditure would keep on declining by one half in each round, till aggregate income is decreased by ₹ 200 crore.

In terms of multiplier formula $-\Delta Y = k(-\Delta I)$, we get $-200 = 2(-100)$. The magnitude of contraction due to backward operation of the multiplier depends upon the value of either MPC or MPS.

Figure 3.23 shows the reverse working of the multiplier.

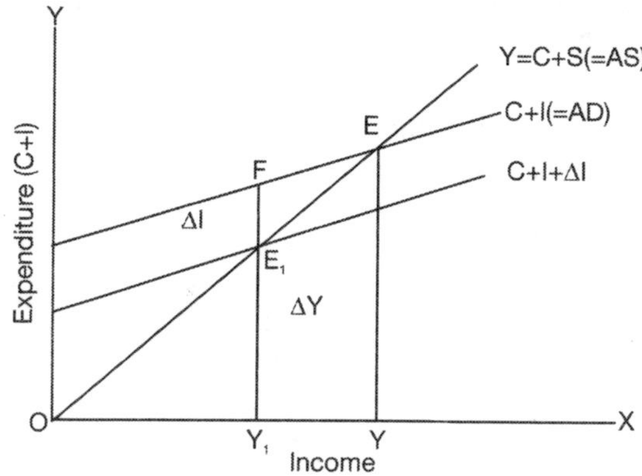

Fig. 3.23: Reverse Working of the Multiplier

As investment declines by $FE_1(\Delta I)$, the equilibrium will move from E to E_1 so income will from Y to Y_1 through multiplier effect.

(ii) Investment Multiplier with Prolonged Expenditure on Investment: So far we have studied the multiplier effect on aggregate income through single expenditure on investment. Keynesian theory of the multiplier is a simultaneous process without time lag or multiplier period. It is a static equilibrium analysis in which the total effect of change in investment on income is instantaneous. So that consumption goods are produced simultaneously and consumption expenditure is also incurred instantaneously. But this is not borne out by facts because a time lag always exists between receipt of income and its expenditure on consumption goods and also in producing consumption goods. In this context, comes the importance of prolonged expenditure on investment. This is also called dynamic multiplier or period multiplier.

The dynamic multiplier relates to the time lags in the process of income generation. The series of adjustment in income and consumption take time-period for the completion of multiplier process. Keynes also agreed that the investment expenditure must be prolonged to keep income to rise continuously in successive period.

It can be explained with the help of an example. The initial investment is ₹ 100 crore and it is also prolonged in successive years and as a result of it the income propagation continued due to the effect of the working of multiplier. Assuming MPC=0.5.

Table 3.10: Working of Dynamic Multiplier or Period Multiplier Time-Period

Time-Period	Increment in investment ΔI	Increment in consumption $\Delta C = C\Delta Y = 0.5$	Increment in in income
t + 1	100	0	100
t + 2	100	50	150
t + 3	100	50+25	175
t + 4	100	50+25+12.50	187.5
....	.....	....	....
....	.....	....	....
....	.....	....	.....
t + n	....	.....	New Level

Table 3.10 shows that if MPC remains constant at 0.5 throughout. An initial increase of ₹ 100 crore of investment will first raise income by ₹ 100 crore in the first period. Out of this ₹ 50 crore is spent on consumption. This will raise income in the second period, i.e. t+2 by ₹ 50 crore and out of this ₹ 25 crore are spent on consumption. Meanwhile ₹ 100 crore investment will be injected in every successive period. Thus, it will increase the total income in each period till it attains the new level. Figure 3.24 illustrates the working of period multiplier.

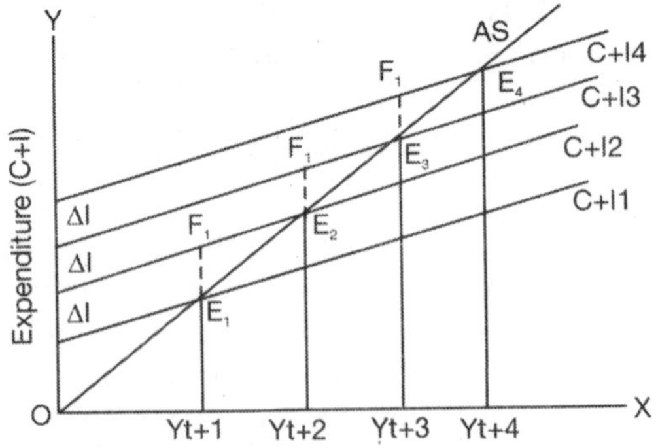

Fig. 3.24: Working of Dynamic Multiplier

In the figure, C+I is the aggregate demand function and AS line is the aggregate supply function. If we begin in period t+1 where with an equilibrium level of income is Yt+1, the investment increased by F_1E_1 will increase the income to Yt+2 in period 't+2'. Thus, the process of increase in investment by same amount in the subsequent time period will generate the income till it reaches the new level of income, i.e. C+I4.

In brief, according to Keynes if the initial investment is not prolonged in successive time-period the initial increased will gradually dry-up so to keep the increase in income continue in the successive periods the injecting of investment should be continued. Since MPC value is constant in short-run the value of multiplier (k) is constant.

3.4.6 Investment Multiplier and Leakages

Under the process of income generation through the investment-multiplier effect if any part of income remains unspent on consumption that is known as 'Leakage'. In other words, the part of income not spent on consumption is called 'Leakage' in the cumulative income stream.

The value of multiplier (k) mainly depends upon the value of MPC but the MPC is oppositely related with the leakages. Higher the value of leakages, lower the value of MPC and on contrary, it is vice versa. For ex: Income is 100 units, leakage from income is 25 units and income spent on consumption is 75 units. So the value of MPC=75% or ¾, and k=1/0.25=4. But when leakage increased to 50 units, the MPC will be ½, or 0.5 so k=1/0.5=2.

Various Forms of Leakages

Following are the various forms of leakages from the income stream.

(i) Idle Cash Balance: People use to keep some part of their increased income as idle cash balance for various purposes. It reduces the marginal propensity to consume that leads to decline in the value of multiplier (k). So it further reduces the income stream.

(ii) Purchase of Old Stocks and Securities: If a part of the new income is used in buying old stocks and securities, instead of consumer goods, the consumption expenditure will fall and its cumulative effect on income will be less than before. In other words, the size of the multiplier will fall with a fall in consumption expenditure as a result of this.

(iii) Repayment of Debts: Income recipients, to pay off old debts, may use a part of the new increment of income. As a consequence, it does not have only effect on consumption. That part of the income goes out of the income stream. In case this part of the increased income is repaid to other creditors who save or hoard it the multiplier process will be arrested.

(iv) Net Imports: If the increased income is spent on the purchase of imported goods, it acts as a leakage out of the domestic income stream. This does not add to domestic income and employment such expenditure fails to effect the consumption of domestic goods. This argument can be extended to net imports when there is an excess of import over exports thereby causing a net outflow of funds to other countries.

(v) Undistributed Profits: If the profits earned by the joint stock companies are not distributed to shareholders in the form of dividend but are kept in the reserve fund, it is a leakage. Undistributed profits with the companies tend to reduce the consumption and hence further expenditure on consumption goods and weaken multiplier process.

(vi) Taxation: Taxation policy weakens the income propagation. Since it affects the marginal propensity to consume of the people, it has inevitable repercussions on the value of the multiplier. Progressive taxes have the effect of lowering the disposable income of the taxpayers and reducing their consumption expenditure. Similarly, commodity taxation tends to raise the prices of goods and a part of the increased income may be lost on higher prices. This further reduces the size of the multiplier.

(vii) Price Inflation: When increased investment leads to price inflation the multiplier effect of increased income may be lost on higher prices. Rise in the prices of consumer goods implies increased expenditure on them. As a result of it the increased income is absorbed in the form of higher prices and the real consumption and income will fall. Thus, price inflation is an important leakage, which tends to dissipate increase in income and consumption on higher prices rather than in increasing output and employment.

Thus, leakages slow down the income propagation and the income generated would be less than the expectation.

3.4.7 Limitations of Multiplier (k)

Investment multiplier works in limited scope. It depends upon marginal propensity to consume and autonomous investment. So the value of multiplier (k) depends upon them in practice. Besides, its working also depends upon the following factors:

(i) **Leakages:** If the leakages to income are more, the value of MPC will be low thus the multiplier effect will also be lower.

(ii) **Availability of Consumer Goods:** If there is scarcity in supply or availability of consumer-goods, the increase in income will lead to savings and thus it will lower the multiplier effect.

(iii) **Multiplier Period:** Keynes income multiplier is a simultaneous or logical multiplier so it does not consider time lag or multiplier period. But according to multiplier period, lower the time period higher will be the value of multiplier (k); higher the time period lover will be k.

(iv) **Full Employment Ceiling:** Any increase in investment at full employment level does not increase the output so the increased income simply raises the prices.

In brief, the multiplier works successfully when the assumptions are held good.

3.4.8 Criticisms of Investment Multiplier

In addition to its several limitations Keynes' multiplier has been criticized by post-Keynesian economists as under as it has certain shortcomings.

(i) **It is a Static Multiplier:** Keynesian logical theory of the multiplier is an instantaneous process without time lag. It is a static multiplier. But Prof. A.H. Hanson suggested three types of multipliers, viz. (a) static or simultaneous or logical multiplier, (b) comparative static multiplier and (c) dynamic multiplier. So

Keynes logical multiplier does not explain 'how income propagates from one equilibrium to other'.

(ii) It Ignores the Effect of Marginal Propensity to Consumption on Induced Investment: One of the weaknesses of the multiplier theory is that it studies the effects of investment an income through changes in consumption expenditure. But it ignores the effect of consumption on investment, which is known as the acceleration principle. Therefore, Keynes' explanation takes one-sided income-generating process. Hicks, Samuelson and others have shown that it is the interaction of the multiplier and the accelerator, which helps to explain the business fluctuations.

(iii) It is Based on Wrong Assumptions: Keynes multiplier theory assumes (a) consumption is the functional outcome of income [C=f (y)] and (b) MPC is less than one (MPC<1) and it is constant in short-run. But modern studies proved that (a) there are other factors influencing on consumption like population, demonstration effect, etc. and (b) in a dynamic economy MPC seldom remains constant.

(iv) It is a Strange Concept: According to Hazlitt, the Keynes' multiplier is a strange concept and Keynesians made more complicated. He calls it a 'myth'. He says there can never be any precise, to be pre-determined or mechanical relationship between investment and income. Thus, he regards it as a "worthless theoretical toy".

(v) It is Mere Arithmetic Multiplier: Prof. Haberler has criticized Keynes' multiplier as tautology. Similarly, Prof. Hansen points out such a coefficient ($k=1/1-\Delta C/\Delta Y$) is a mere arithmetic multiplier (i.e. truism) but it is not a true behaviour multiplier based on a behaviour pattern that establishes a verifiable relations between consumption and income.

(vi) Assumption of Less than Full Employment is Criticized: Keynes' analysis is based on an unrealistic assumption that is existence unemployment in the economy. The theory is not applicable to full employment economy.

(vii) It is Self Contradictory: Hazlitt pointed out another pitfall in the multiplier theory that is the theory assumes that the entire fraction of community's income which is not spent on consumption is hoarded so it is not invested. The propensity to consume determines the size of the multiplier only on the perception that what is not spent on consumption is not spent on anything at all. It is hoarded and not invested.

This is contradictory to Keynes own statement that the saving and investment are not only equal, but also identical. In other words, what is not spent means what is saved must necessarily be invested so that saving and investment are equal. But the acceptance of the multiplier concept gives rise to the problem of inequality between saving and investment according to Hazlitt. Thus, Keynes' concept of the multiplier is not in conformity with his own definitions of saving and investment given in *General Theory*.

(viii) Keynes Multiplier Theory Establishes a Linear Relation between Consumption and Income: It assumed that MPC is less than one and constant in short-run and thus it has established the linear relation between consumption and income. The modern empirical studies proved that the relation between them is complicated and non-linear. Gardner Ackley has pointed out "the relationship does not run simply from current income to current consumption. But it involves some complex average of past and expected income and consumption".

However, in spite of its limitations and criticisms, the multiplier principle has considerable degree of practical applicability to economic problems.

3.4.9 Importance or Significance of Investment Multiplier

Multiplier is one of the important contributions of Keynes to the income and employment theory. Richard Goodwin comments "Lord Keynes did not discover the multiplier; that honour goes to Mr. R.F. Kahn. But he gave it the role it plays today by transforming it from an instrument for the analysis of road building into one for the analysis of income building.... It set a fresh wind blowing through the structure of economic thought". Its applicability can be illustrated as follows.

(i) It Highlights the Importance of Investment in Income and Employment Theory: Since the consumption function is stable during the short-run, fluctuations in income and employment are due to fluctuations in investment. A fall in investment leads to a cumulative decline in income and employment by the multiplier process and vice versa. Thus, it underlines the importance of investment in the process of income propagation.

(ii) It Helps to Explain Business Fluctuations: The multiplier throws a spotlight on the different phases of the trade cycle. Trade cycle represents periodic fluctuation in aggregate economic activity consisting of income, employment, output and the general price level. For example, when investment declines, it will lead to decline in income and employment cumulatively which will lead to recession and ultimately to depression. On the contrary, rise in investment leads to revival and boom. Thus, multiplier is an indispensable tool to explain the trade cycles.

(iii) It Helps for Formulation of Economic Policies: Multiplier is an important tool in the hands of modern states for formulating economic policies. Keynes suggests the government to undertake the autonomous investment to raise income and employment. Thus, this principle shows the necessity of state intervention in economic affairs.

In brief, Keynes' multiplier presupposes intervention of the government in economic affairs. It is a revolutionary contribution to the world of advanced economic doctrines.

3.5 MODEL QUESTIONS

2-Marks Questions

1. What is effective demand?
2. What is aggregate demand?
3. What is aggregate supply?
4. What do you mean by autonomous consumption?
5. What is induced consumption?
6. Give the central them of Keynes' Income and Theory.
7. Mention Keynes' two conditions of equilibrium.

8. Give any two criticisms of Keynes income and employment theory.
9. In consumption equation, C=a+b(y), a=₹100, b=0.5 so calculate the value of c when y=1000.
10. What is propensity to consume?
11. When C=400 and y=600, find out the value of Average Propensity to Consume (APC).
12. When y=800, c=600 and s=200, find out the value of APC and APS.
13. When APC=0.7, find out the value of MPS.
14. What is Marginal Propensity to Consume (MPC)?
15. When Y_1=200, Y_2=600, C_1=180, C_2=340, S_1=20 and S_2=60, find out the value of MPC and MPS.
16. What is consumption function?
17. Mention any two subjective factors influencing consumption.
18. Mention any two objective factors influencing consumption.
19. State any two importance of consumption function.
20. Why does MPC remain constant in short-run?
21. What is investment?
22. State the differences between induced and autonomous investments.
23. What is investment function?
24. What do you mean by Marginal Efficiency of Capital?
25. What are the determinants of MEC?
26. If Q=100, r=8%, find out the value of Cr or supply price of capital asset.
27. What is investment multiplier?
28. What do you mean by multiplier effect?
29. If MPC=3/4, find out the value of MPS.
30. If MPC=4/5, find out the value of k.

31. State the difference between simultaneous and period multipliers.
32. Mention any two assumptions of multiplier theory.
33. What do you mean by leakage from income-stream?
34. Mention any two leakages.
35. Mention any two limitations of multiplier theory.
36. If I=150, k=4, calculate the value of Y.
37. Mention any two criticisms of multiplier.
38. Give any two importance of multiplier theory.

5-Marks Questions

1. Write a note on effective demand.
2. State Keynes' conditions of full employment.
3. Write a note on significance of Keynes' income and employment theory.
4. Draw a summarized chart of Keynes' income and employment theory.
5. Give a diagrammatic illustration of working of Keynes' income and employment theory.
6. Write a note on criticisms on Keynes' income and employment theory.
7. Find out superiorities of Keynes' income and employment theory.
8. Write note on consumption schedule.
9. Write note on properties of Keynes' psychological law of consumption.
10. Write a note on assumptions and implications of Keynes' consumption theory.
11. Write a note on APC and APS.
12. Write a note on MPC and MPS.
13. Write a note on subjective factors influencing consumption.

14. Write a note on objective factors influencing consumption.
15. Write a note on importance of consumption function.
16. Write a note on autonomous and induced investment.
17. Write a note on marginal efficiency of capital.
18. Explain in brief supply price of capital asset.
19. Explain in brief demand price of capital asset.
20. Discuss in brief the factors influencing marginal efficiency of capital.
21. Write a note on MEC and expectations.
22. Explain in brief the working of income multiplier.
23. Write a note on income multiplier and leakages.
24. Write a note on criticisms of income multiplier.
25. Write a note on importance of income multiplier.

10-Marks Questions

1. Explain Keynes' income and employment theory.
2. What is 'Effective Demand'? Explain its determinants.
3. Critically examine Keynes' income and employment theory.
4. Explain the consumption function.
5. What is consumption function? Explain APC and MPC.
6. Explain the investment function.
7. What is MEC? Explain its determinants.
8. Discuss the Keynes' income multiplier theory.
9. What is income multiplier? Explain its working.

4

Acceleration Principle

4.1 ACCELERATION PRINCIPLE

The income propagation depends upon both the multiplier effect and the accelerator effect. The principle of acceleration is not dealt by Keynes in his income and employment theory. Acceleration is not a Keynesian concept. Keynes ignored it deliberately saying that investment multiplier is enough to explain income propagation.

The principle of acceleration is another important tool of economic analysis. It is older than the multiplier. T.N. Carver was the earliest economist who recognized the relationship between changes in consumption and net investment in 1903. But it was Aftalion who analyzed this principle in detail in 1909. J.M. Clark first introduced the term "Acceleration Principle" itself into economics in 1917 and therefore generally it is associated with his name. Later Ragnar Frisch, J.R. Hicks, Paul Samuelson and R.F. Harrod further developed it in relation to the business cycles. R.F. Harrod was the first man to create keen interest to use 'Acceleration Principle' as a tool of business cycle analysis.

4.1.1 Meaning and Definitions

The aggregate demand consists of demand for consumption goods and demand for capital goods so it is written as:

AD= C+I, where AD=aggregate demand, C = demand for consumption goods and I=demand for capital goods

Keynes' income multiplier considers the consumption side. According to Keynes, the change in autonomous investment directly leads to change in income first then as a consequence of it consumption and savings will be changed. The change in consumption results into change in demand for capital goods to undertake the production of consumer goods. It brings more income to the investors so induced investment will be increased. Thus, this chain effect can be written as: $\Delta Ia \rightarrow \Delta Y \rightarrow \Delta C \rightarrow \Delta Ii$, therefore, $Ii = f(Y)$.

The acceleration considers the induced investment side. It explains the change in consumption leads to change in investment which generates income (GNP). So the acceleration is defined by Prof. Kurihar as "The accelerator coefficient is the ratio between induced investment and an initial change in consumptions expenditure". In other words, the ratio between the net change in consumption and the induced investment is known as acceleration co-efficient or 'Relation'.

Symbolically, it can be written as: $v=\Delta I/\Delta C$. Here v= acceleration or relation, ΔI=change in induced investment and ΔC= change in consumption. For example, if $\Delta I=100$ and $\Delta C=10$, the value of $v=100/10=10$. It means the production of ₹ 10 worth consumption goods requires ₹ 100 worth capital goods. Therefore, the value of 'Relation' (v) depends upon the capital: output ratio, i.e. K/O, K = capital and O = output. Therefore, $v = \Delta I/\Delta C$ or K/ O. Further the value of v influences on income generation.

Thus, according J.R. Hicks, accelerator 'v' = $\Delta I/\Delta Y$ or the accelerator is equal to capital output ratio. It depends upon the relevant change in output (ΔY) and the change in investment (ΔI). It shows that the demand for capital goods is not derived from consumer goods alone but any direct demand for national output.

In an economy the required stock of capital depends upon the change in the demand for output. Any change in output will lead to a change in capital stock. This change equals 'v' time the change in output. Thus, $\Delta I = v\Delta Y$, where 'v' is the accelerator. If a machine has a value of ₹ 100 lakh and produces output worth ₹ 10 lakh, then the value of 'v' is 10. An entrepreneur who wishes to increase his output by ₹ 10 lakh every year must invest ₹ 100 lakh on the machines, i.e. $\Delta I = v\Delta Y$ or ₹ 100 lakh = 10 × 10 lakh.

This is applicable to whole economy. If the value of the accelerator is greater than one, more capital will be required per unit of output. So, the increase in net investment is greater than the increase in output. Gross investment, consists of replacement investment plus net investment, i.e. GI = NI+RI here GI = gross investment, NI = net investment, and RI = replace investment. Assuming replacement investment as constant, the gross investment will vary with the level of investment corresponding to each level of output.

The accelerator principle can be expressed in the form of Broman equation as:

$$I_{gt} = v\,(Y_t - Y_{t-1}) + R$$
$$= v\Delta Y_t + R$$

Here I_{gt} = gross investment in period t, v = accelerator, Y_t = national output in period t, Y_{t-1} = national output in the previous period (t–1) and R = replacement investment.

Replacement of old and worn-out capital good is called 'replacement cost' or 'replacement investment'. The value of replacement investment is depending upon the life-span of capital good. Replacement investment (RI) may be calculated as: 1/life-span of capital good × 100 = RI. For example, if life-span of a machine is 100 years then RI = 1/10 × 100 = 10%. Higher the life-span, lower will be the demand for capital good for replacement; lower the life-span, higher will be the demand for capital good for replacement purpose.

The gross investment equation tells that gross investment during period t depends on the change in output (Y) from period t–1 to period t multiplied by the accelerator (v) plus replacement investment R.

In order to arrive at net investment (I_{nt}), R must be deducted from both sides of the equation so that the net investment in period t is $I_{nt} = v\,(Y_t - Y_{t-1}) = v\Delta Yt$. For example, if ΔY_t = ₹ 10, v = 10, the value of net investment, I_{nt} = 10×10=100.

This equation is nothing but $\Delta I = v\Delta Y$, since $\Delta Y = Yt-Yt-1$ Further there is little difference between $\Delta I = v\Delta Y$ as defined by Hicks and $\Delta I = v\Delta C$ or $= \Delta I/\Delta C$ as defined by Samuelson and others. J.R. Hicks takes the increase in final output (ΔY) while Samuelson takes the increase in demand for consumer goods (ΔC).

In Hicks model net investment (I_{nt}) $= v(Y_t-Y_{t-1})$ while in Samuelson's model $I_{nt} = v(C_t-C_{t-1})$. It has become customary to explain the acceleration principle in terms of final output (Y). If $Y_t > Y_{t-1}$, net investment is positive during period t on the other hand if $Y_t < Y_{t-1}$, net investment is negative or there is disinvestments in period t.

4.1.2 Assumptions

The working of acceleration principle is based on the following assumptions:

(i) **Full Utilization of Capital Stock of the Economy:** There is no excess or idle capacity in plants. If there is under utilization of plants or machineries, any increase in demand for consumer goods will not raise the demand for capital goods because the existing plants or machines will be used to produce consumer goods.

(ii) **The Capital:Output Ratio should Remain Constant:** There is no change in technology or methods of production.

(iii) **The Producers should Add New Plants or Machines:** Even if the demand for consumer goods is temporary or short-lived, the producers should add new machines to capital stock for production of consumer goods.

(iv) **No Limit to Investment:** It is also assumed that there is no limit to the investment.

(v) **Supply of Capital Goods should be Perfectly Elastic:** The supply of machineries or plants should be perfectly elastic. Otherwise, the acceleration principle cannot work.

(vi) **Easy and Uninterrupted Supply of Resources:** The industry is in a fluid state and there is no time lag in the supply of factors so that "finished goods are turned out as fast as wanted and materials and means of production are instantly supplied as fast as the process of finishing requires them".

(vii) Output should Increase as Investment Increases: It also assume, that the increase in output should be accompanied by the increase in investment.

4.1.3 Working of Acceleration Principle

The working of acceleration principle is explained with the help of a hypothetical example: Ceiling-fan is a consumer good and machines required to produce the ceiling-fan are capital goods. At a given technology, 100 machines are required to produce 10 ceiling-fans so the capital:output ratio is 100:10, thus the value of v =10. The life-span of the machine is 10 years so 10 per cent of machines are to be replaced every year. The demand for ceiling is changing.

Table 4.1: Working of the Acceleration Principle

Time-Period (t)	Output (Ceiling-fan) (Y)	Total Required Capital (I) v=10×Y	Replacement Investment (R)	Net Investment (I_n) $v(Y_n - Y_{n-1})$	Gross investment (I_g)
0	10	100	10	00	10
1	11	110	10	10	20
2	15	150	11	40	51
3	15	150	15	00	15
4	14	140	15	–10	05
5	11	110	14	–30	–16
6	08	80	11	–20	–09
7	07	70	08	–10	–02
8	05	50	07	–20	–13
9	01	10	05	–40	–35
10	00	00	01	–10	–09

Table 4.1 explains the changes in total output, capital stock, net investment, and gross investment over ten periods. Assuming the value of acceleration v=10, the required capital stock in each period is 10 times the corresponding output of that period as shown in column (3) of the table. The replacement investment is assumed to be 10 per cent of the capital stock in just preceding period. Net investment in column (5) equals v times the change in output between one period and the preceding period. For example, net investment in period $t_2 = v\,(Y_2 - Y_1) = 10(15-11) = 10(4) = 40$.

The table also explains that the demand for capital good cannot fall to zero because there is always demand for it for replacement purpose. J.M. Clark had used this tool to explain two things: (i) the derived demand for capital good is highly sensitive means demand for capital good fluctuates more than demand for consumer good and (ii) the extent of acceleration effect depends on ratio between new demand for investment and replacement investment that depends upon life-span of capital good.

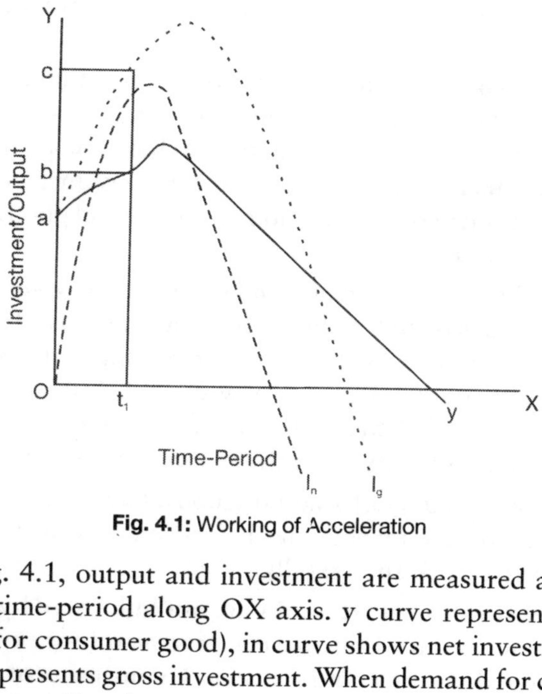

Fig. 4.1: Working of Acceleration

In Fig. 4.1, output and investment are measured along OY axis and time-period along OX axis. y curve represents output (demand for consumer good), in curve shows net investment and I_g curve represents gross investment. When demand for consumer goods increased by ab at t_1 period and as a result of it the demand for capital goods (investment) is increased by ac. The distance ac is the 'Acceleration-Effect'.

4.1.4 Limitations and Criticisms

The accelerator principle has certain limitations so it is criticized by economists as following:

(i) **The Capital:** output ratio need not remain constant: The accelerator principle assumed that the capital output ratio should remain constant. But, in the modern dynamic world, the inventions and improvements in techniques of production will lead to capital; output ratio.

(ii) **The Accelerator Principle Assumes the Availability of Resources:** The resources like fund, raw materials, etc. should be available in the economy. But there is uncertainty in supply of resources at fair prices in the economy. The non-availability of resources like funds will limit the working of acceleration principle.

(iii) **Existence of Excess Capacity in the Economy:** The principle assumes that there is no unused or idle capacity in plants. If there is under-utilization of some machines or plants in the economy, an increase in the demand for consumer goods will not lead to the increase in demand for new capital goods. In such a situation accelerator cannot work.

(iv) **The Short-term Changes in Demand for Consumer Good does Lead to Permanent Change in Investment:** In case the demand for consumer goods is expected to be temporary, the producers will not take up investment on new capital. Instead they may meet the increased demand by working the existing capital equipment more intensity. Therefore, acceleration will not work.

(v) **Inelastic Supply of Capital Goods:** Generally, the supply of capital goods like machineries is inelastic so it is difficult for acceleration to work successfully.

(vi) **The Investment Decisions are not Influenced by Demand Alone:** The accelerator principle neglects the role of expectations in decision-making by entrepreneurs. The investment decisions are not influenced by demand alone. They are also influenced by future expectations like stock market changes, political developments, international events, economic climate, etc. Therefore, regardless of the present state of demand entrepreneurs will not increase present capacity unless their future anticipation warrants the step.

(vii) **Accelerator Principle Neglects the Role of Technological Factors in Investment:** Technological changes may be either capital saving or labour saving. They may therefore either reduce or increase the volume of investment. Further capital equipment may be bulky and the employment of additional plant is justified only when output has risen considerably. This factor is more important in the working of accelerator.

(viii) Long-run Investment is Made Well in Advance: There are several cases where investments do not await changes in the rate of consumption. The long-term investments are made well in advance of an expected change in the rate of consumption. Investments in such cases do not follow changes in consumption.

4.1.5 Significance of Accelerator

Despite of criticisms and limitations, the accelerator principle is more realistic than the multiplier theory. Its importance can be assessed as follows:

(i) Accelerator Helps to Understand the Process of Income Generation in a Clearer and a More Scientific Manner: The concept of multiplier does not explain the entire process of income generation. It explains only a part of it but the remaining other part is explained by accelerator. Thus, it is necessary to integrate the multiplier with the accelerator to explain the entire process of national income generation.

(ii) It Adequately Explains why Investment Goods Industries Fluctuate More Violently than the Consumer Goods Industries: It also explains why small changes in demand for consumption goods lead to considerable changes in investment goods industries. In other words, it explains that the demand for the investment goods during any period results from the derived demand for consumption goods over the period.

(iii) It is an Indispensable Tool to Analysis of Cyclical Fluctuations: The accelerator principle has become an indispensable tool to analysis the cyclical fluctuations of business activity in the economy. Prof. J.R. Hicks and Prof. R.F. Harrod developed their theories of business cycle on the basis of accelerator principle.

In brief, the acceleration principle is theoretically sound and it has practical significance.

4.1.6 Comparison between Multiplier and Accelerator

The comparison between multiplier and accelerator is explained as under:

(i) Difference in Effect: Multiplier (k) shows the effect of the change in investment on income and employment whereas the accelerator (v) shows the effect of the change in consumption on investment.

(ii) Difference in Dependency: In multiplier theory, the consumption depends upon investment whereas in accelerator, the investment depends upon consumption.

(iii) Difference in Determinants: The determinant of the value of multiplier (k) is the value of marginal propensity to consume (MPC) or marginal propensity to save (MPS). But the accelerator coefficient depends upon the durability of capital goods or machines and capital:output ratio.

(iv) Difference in Influencing Factor: The multiplier is influenced by psychological factors. It means multiplier is influenced by propensity to consume which is determined by psychological factors like consumer's tastes and habits. But the accelerator is influenced by technical factors. In other words, the value of accelerator is influenced by technology which determines capital:output ratio. It is all technological aspect.

However, the integration of both will give us complete picture of the income generated through initial increase in investment.

4.2 INTERACTION BETWEEN MULTIPLIER (k) AND ACCELERATOR (v): SUPER MULTIPLIER

4.2.1 Meaning

We have studied the working of 'Multiplier' (k) and 'Accelerator or Relation' (v) separately. The accelerator itself is not perhaps more forceful but recently it received more importance in the analysis of business cycle theory by its alliance with multiplier theory. The interaction of the acceleration with the multiplier is capable, under certain circumstances, of generating continuous cyclical fluctuations. Economists like P.A. Samuelson, J.R. Hicks, R.F. Harrod and Alvin H. Hanson have made fairly successful attempts to integrate the two parallel concepts and thus introduced certain remarkable improvements. Therefore, it is quite interesting and useful to analyze the combined effects of multiplier and acceleration on national income propagation. This combined effect of multiplier (k) and acceleration is called 'Leverage-Effect' by A.H. Hanson.

According to Hanson, the leverage-effect explains the mutual relation between investment and consumption. The injection of autonomous investment has a magnified effect on total employment and income and consequently a magnified effect on the demand for consumer goods (the multiplier). This in turn leads to an increase in investment to produce to meet the demand for consumer goods (the accelerator). These derivative-investments again activate the multiplier mechanism and magnify the increase in employment and income which leads to a new wave of induced investment.

According to R. Khafizov, a Soviet Economist, Prof. Hanson combined 'k' with 'v' because the concept of multiplier provides only a one-sided picture of the mutual dependence of investment and consumption that is consumption grows as a consequence of investment. It completely disregards the fact that the investment itself depends upon consumption. So he integrated the other side that is acceleration with multiplier to explain the mutual dependence of investment and consumption.

Economists like Harrod, Hicks, Samuelson and Kurihara have also made attempts to combine these parallel concepts. Prof. J.R. Hicks has combined both the principles mathematically to find out the total effect of initial investment on income and he called it 'Super-multiplier'. Hicks' 'Super Multiplier', denoted as $k\Delta$, the combined effect of autonomous investment and induced investment on the income propagation. He says that if the value of $k\Delta$ is known, we can find out the equilibrium level of income correspondence to the given level of autonomous investment. Given the value of $k\Delta$, higher the autonomous investment, higher the value of income propagation.

4.2.2 Mathematical Illustration of Hicks' 'Super Multiplier'

Hicks used the following income equation to arrive at the value of super multiplier ($k\Delta$):

Y=C+I, where Y=Aggregate Income, C=Aggregate Consumption, I=Aggregate Investment.

Since aggregate investment consists of (i) autonomous investment, denoted by 'Ia', and (ii) induced investment, denoted by 'Ii', so equation (1) can be written as:

$$Y=C=Ia=Ii \quad ...(1)$$

It is known fact that C=f(Y), consumption is the outcome of income, a change in income leads to a change in consumption, i.e. MPC (Marginal Propensity to consume or CΔ/ΔY).

Similarly, induced investment (Ii) is also related with the change in income (ΔY) which is called 'Marginal Propensity to Invest' (MPI).

∴ C=f(Y) or C=Ca + b(Y), where Ca= Autonomous Consumption, c(Y)=Induced Consumption

Similarly Ii= d(Y)

∴ Y=Ca+cY+Ia+dY......(1) since Ys are brought at one side:

$$Y-cY-dY= Ca+Ia$$

$$\text{Or} \quad Y(1-c-d) = Ca+Ia$$

$$\text{Or} \quad Y = \frac{Ca + Ia}{1 - c - d} \quad ...(2)$$

If there is any change in autonomous investment, it will lead to the new level of income. It is written as:

$$Y' = \frac{Ca + Ia + \Delta Ia}{1 - c - d} \quad ...(3)$$

By deducting Eq. (2) from Eq. (3), we get the value of 'Super Multiplier' (k′).

$$\Delta Y = Y' - Y = \frac{Ca + Ia + \Delta Ia}{1 - c - d} - \frac{Ca + Ia}{1 - c - d} = \frac{\Delta Ia}{1 - c - d}$$

$$\therefore \quad \frac{\Delta Y}{\Delta Ia} = \frac{1}{1 - c - d} = k' \text{ (Super Multiplier)}$$

k′ is different from Keynes' k is that Keynes' income multiplier (k) value depends on the value of MPC whereas Hicks' super multiplier (k′) value depends on combined effect of k and v means MPC and MPI.

Further Hicks said that the value of c (MPC)and d (MPI) are positive that is $c \leq 1$ and $d \leq 1$ so $c+d < 1$.

In brief, the change in autonomous investment leads to the change in income but the magnitude of change in income depends on the value of k′.

The following numerical example helps to understand the difference between Keynes' multiplier effect and Hicks' super multiplier effect.

Assume the value of c (MPC)=0.6, d(PMI)=0.2 and the change in autonomous investment (ΔIa)= 100 crore.

(i) Keynes' income multiplier: $\Delta Y = \Delta Ia \times k$

$$\therefore \quad k = \frac{1}{1-c} = \frac{1}{1-0.6} = 2.5$$ by substituting the values,

$\Delta Y = 100 \times 2.5 =$ ₹ 250 crore.

(ii) Hicks' super multiplier: $\Delta Y = \Delta Ia \times k'$

$$\therefore \quad k' = \frac{1}{1-c-d} = \frac{1}{1-0.6-0.2} = 5$$ by substituting the values,

$\Delta Y = 100 \times 2.5 =$ ₹ 500 crore.

4.2.3 Working of Super Multiplier

The working of super multiplier or the combined effect of c and d is explained in Table 4.2 with the help of above numerical example.

In the first period, t+1, initial investment of ₹ 100 crore is injected into the economy but there is no immediate induced consumption or investment. In period t+2 induced consumption of 60 takes place out of the income 100 of the previous period because the marginal propensity to consume is 0.60. There is an induced investment of 20 out of 100 incomes (d = 0.2). The increase in income from period t+1 to t+2 is (60 + 20) = 80. The increase in income in different periods can be calculated as:

Table 4.2: Working of Super Multiplier

(₹ in crore)

Period	Initial investment (ΔIa)	Induced consumption (C=0.6)	Induced investment (d=0.2)	Increase in income (ΔY)
t + 1	100	0	0	100
t + 2	...	60	20	80
t + 3	...	48	16	64
t + 4	...	38.4	12.8	51.2
t + 5	...	30.72	10.24	40.96
t + 6	...	24.58	8.19	32.77
t+7	...	19.66	6.55	26.21
So on	...	...	...	...
t + n	100	250	150	500

$$\Delta Y_{t+3} = C\Delta Y_{t+2} + dY_{t+2} = 0.60 \times 80 + 0.2 \times 80 = 64$$

$$\Delta_{Yt+4} = C\Delta Y_{t+3} + d\Delta Y_{t+4} = 0.60 \times 64 + 0.2 \times 64 = 51.2.$$

This cumulative process of income propagation continues till in the period t+n where the induced consumption and induced investment will become difficult for further division. If we add up the increase in consumption, investment and income from period t+1 to t+n the income increases to ₹ 500 crore, total consumption ₹ 250 crore and total investment to ₹ 150 crore given the initial investment of ₹ 100 crore.

The combined effect of multiplier and accelerator on the aggregate income over the period may be shown in Fig. 4.2.

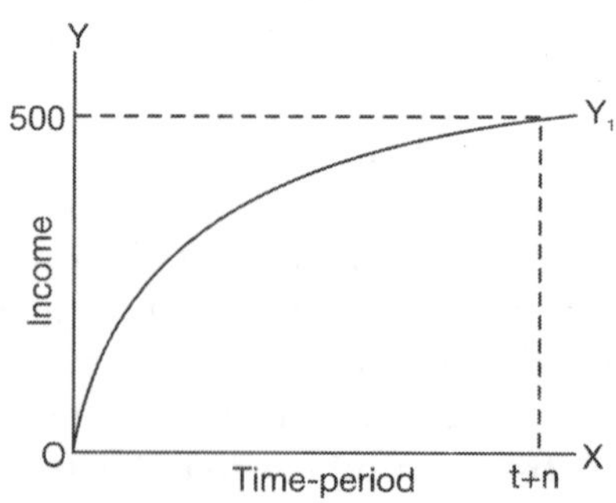

Fig. 4.2: Combined Effect of Multiplier and Acceleration

The dynamic path of increase in income is shown by Y_1 curve in the figure. Income is measured along OY axis and time period along OX axis. The curve rises with time and reaches the new equilibrium level of income Y_1 and flattens out. It indicates that income increases at a decreasing rate.

Interaction between Multiplier (k) and Accelerator (v)

The interaction between multiplier and acceleration results into the income propagation with cyclical fluctuations which creates business cycles in the economy. It can be explained with the help of example. Suppose MPC = ½ or 0.5 and the accelerator coefficient (v) = 2. Given the same assumptions and the initial investment of ₹ 100 crore, let us study how changes in income take place. Table 4.3 explains the process of income propagation.

Table 4.3: Multiplier and Accelerator Interaction

(₹ in crore)

Period (t)	Initial investment (Ia)	Induced consumption (MPC=0.5)	Induced investment (v=2)	Increase in income
0	0	0	0	0
t+1	100	-	-	100
t+2	100	50	100	250
t+3	100	125	150	375
t+4	100	187.50	125	412.5
t+5	100	206.25	37.5	343.75
t+6	100	171.88	–68.74	203.14
t+7	100	101.57	140.62	60.95
t+8	100	30.48	–142.18	–11.73
t+9	100	–05.48	–72.66	21.49
t+10	100	10.75	33.20	143.95

Table 4.3 revels that in period t+1 there is an increase of ₹ 100 crore by the amount of initial investment. This increase in income leads to a rise in consumption of ₹ 50 crore (column 3) in period t+2 because the value of MPC is 0.5. This rise in consumption induces investment of ₹ 100 crore = 50 × 2 (column 4), the accelerator coefficient being 2. And the income increases to ₹ 250 crore (column 2+3+4). This increased income in turn leads to an increase in consumption of ₹ 125 crore (column 3)

being one half of ₹ 250 crore as MPC is 0.5. But consumption in period t is a function of income of the previous period. Therefore, the actual increase in consumption in period t+3 is the difference between consumption in period t+3 and t+2, i.e. ₹ 125 – 50 = ₹ 75 crore. If we multiply this increase in consumption by the value of the accelerator 2, we get induced investment of ₹ 150 crore = 75 × 2 (column 4) in period t+3. Thus, the total of columns 2+3+4 gives increase in income of ₹ 375 crore in period t+3. This process repeats itself over the period. The increase in income is the highest in period t+4 (₹ 412.5 crore) which shows the peak of the cycle. Thereafter it starts falling till it reaches the bottom or trough, when income is ₹ –11.73 crore in period t+8. From period t+9, it again starts rising which shows the revival phase of the cycle.

This behaviour of income as a result of the combined operation of the multiplier and the accelerator reveals that income first rises, and then falls and again it rises at constant amplitudes. This behaviour is shown in Fig. 4.3.

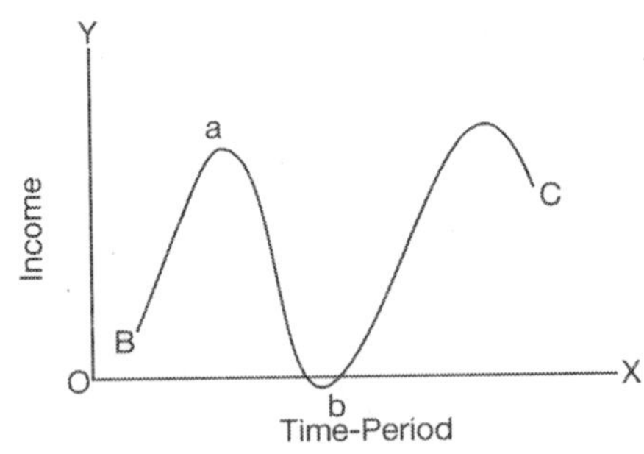

Fig. 4.3: Combined Effect of k and v to Generate Business Cycle

In this figure, above, OX axis measures time period and OY axis the national income. The curve BC represents the actual process of income generation and the cyclical fluctuations in it that shows the 'Leverage Effect'. The national income rises from ₹ 100 crore to a peak level of ₹ 412.5 crore (i.e. a) but later declines from ₹ 412.50 crore to ₹ –11.73 crore in the period t+8 (i.e. b) and reaches the bottom or slump. After point b, it starts again to rise and thus completes the business cycle.

The nature of such fluctuations or oscillations or amplitudes of business cycle depends upon the value of multiplier and acceleration.

Why does the Cumulative Process Come to an End Before a Complete Collapse or Before Full Employment?

This crucial question will be answered by marginal propensity to consume which is less than one or unity. Prof. Hansen says that the rise in income is progressively slowed down on account of the fact that a large part of the increase in income in each successive period is not spent on consumption. This results into a decline in the volume of induced investment and when such decline exceeds the increase in induced consumption, the decline in income sets in. In other words, the marginal propensity to save (MPS) stops income expansion process.

4.2.4 Importance of Interaction between k and v

The following are the importance of the study of interaction between multiplier and acceleration.

(i) It helps to have a tool to analyze accurately the nature of cyclical process.

(ii) It is useful to explain the turning points in business cycle.

(ii) It shows that government can influence on economic activities through public expenditure.

4.2.5 Limitations of Interaction

No doubt, the leverage-effect or interaction k and v explains the income propagation and business cycle but it has certain limitations.

(i) It is a Great Illusion: The interaction assures that it is very easy to lift the economy from the bottom of depression by simply injecting autonomous investment. The autonomous investment would stimulate consumption through multiplier effect which further induces the investment as a result of it national income would grow continuously. But it is a great illusion because in actual practice the leverage-effect does not raise national income higher and higher. It explains only the cyclical fluctuations in national income.

(ii) It is not the Only Factor: There are several other factors which also explain the cyclical fluctuations in national income.

4.3 SAVINGS AND INVESTMENT CONTROVERSY

Savings means the part of income not spent on consumption. On the other hand, investment means the spending on capital goods or assets or process of production or business. Economists believe that there is equality between savings and investment. But there are difference of opinions about the equality between savings and investment. These are studies as under:

(A) The Classical View: According to classical economists, savings is virtue to both individual and community. They say that increase in consumption by a person not only makes a person himself poor but it also makes the nation poor. Thus, savings is virtue because it raises investment, income savings and consumption also.

The classicals believe that there is always equality between savings and investment at full employment level. They further said that both savings and investment are a function of the rate of interest. Algebraically, it can be expressed as under:

$$S=f(r)$$

$$I= f(r)$$

where S = savings, I = investment and r = rate of interest.

$$\therefore \quad S = I$$

Any change in rate of interest (r) will disturb the equilibrium in short-run but in long-run the automatic adjustment between demand and supply forces will restore the equilibrium rate of interest and S=I will be restored. It is shown in Fig. 4.4.

In the figure, the quantity of demand and supply of saving and investment are measured along OX axis and the rate of interest along OY axis. S is the savings curve and I is the investment curve. Both S and I curves are intersected each other at E and the equilibrium rate of interest is or and savings and investment are equal (S=I). If the rate of interest increases to r_1 in short-run, investment (Q_1 or r_1a) will become less than savings (Q_2 or r_1b). But in long-run the equality between savings and investment will take place through adjustment in demand and supply of savings or investment and the equilibrium rate of interest (r) will be restored.

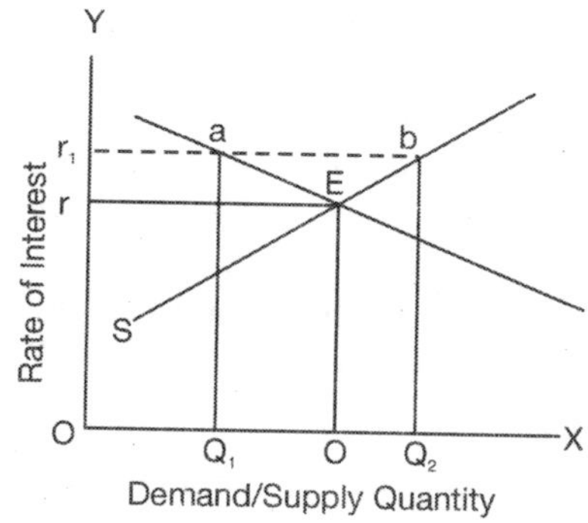

Fig. 4.4: Saving and Investment

Classical Paradox of Thriftiness

Thrift means to limit or reduce the consumption. According to classical economists, the increase in consumption eventually reduces the level of consumption which is called 'Classical Paradox of Thriftiness'. It can be shown as:

$$\uparrow C \rightarrow \downarrow S \rightarrow \downarrow I \rightarrow \downarrow Y \rightarrow \downarrow C$$

According to this paradox of thrift, the increase in consumption initially reduces savings which results into decline in investment and income that ends in decline in consumption. It leads to depression. So they said that the consumption should be reduced which ultimately ends in increase in consumption and prosperity.

(B) **Keynes View:** Keynes in his famous book *General Theory of Employment, Interest and Money* discussed the relation between saving and investment in two senses. They are discussed as under:

(i) Savings (S) and Investment (I) Both are Equal by Definition: According to Keynes, by definition, there is always equality between savings and investment. It is proven by using income and expenditure equations:

Income-Equation: $Y = C + S$

Expenditure-Equation: $Y = C + I$

By substituting the value of Y in either equation, we get

$$C + S = C + I$$

$$\therefore S = I$$

(ii) There can be Divergence Between S and I: According to Keynes, the savings and investment need not be equal to each other in practice. It is because savings are done by some people and the investments are done by some other people. Besides, the determinants of savings are different from the determinants of investment. So by functionally (f) both are different:

$$S = f(Y)$$

It means savings (S) depends upon the level of income (Y).

$$I = f(r, MEC)$$

It means investment depends upon rate of interest (r) and marginal efficiency of capital MEC).

$$\therefore S = I$$

To clarify the convergence relation between savings and investment, Keynes divided savings and investment in two types as below:

(i) Planned Savings and Planned Investment: They are also known as 'ex-ante or intended' savings and investment. The people plan to save some part of their income for purposes like to meet future needs, for children, old age, etc. Higher the plan more will be the supply of ex-ante savings.

The business people, producers and investors plan to undertake investment for the purpose of earning profit or rate of return of capital and interest. Such investments are called ex-ante or planned investments.

Since ex-ante savings group of people are different from ex-ante investors, both are need not be equal. But they are equal only at the point of equilibrium.

(ii) Realized Savings and Realized Investment: They are also known as 'ex-post or unintended or unplanned' savings and investment. These are the actual savings and investment so they are necessarily equal at the point of equilibrium. Actual savings determines actual investment.

Diagrammatic Illustration

Both planned and realized savings and investment are illustrated in Fig. 4.5.

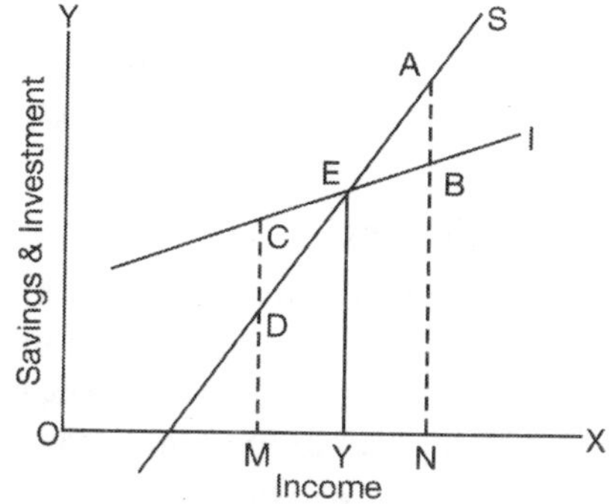

Fig. 4.5: Planned and Realized Savings and Investment

In the figure, S is savings curve and I is investment curve. Savings and investment are measured along OY axis and the income along OX axis. Both curves are intersected each other at E so E is equilibrium point where:

RS=RI and PS=PI

where RS= Realized Savings, RI= Realized Investment,
PS= Planned Savings and PI= Planned Investment.

Both types of savings and investments are equal when income is OY. The RS and RI are found only at E point where income is OY. But at other than OY income we found PS=PI. For example, (i) When income is OM, PS<PI that is MD (savings) is less than CM (investment). (ii) When income is ON, PS>PI that is AN (savings) is greater than BN (investment).

The disequilibrium between planned savings and planned investment will create changes in economic activities and finally will take the economy to either contraction or expansion. These possibilities are studied as under:

(i) If PS>PI, it takes the economy to contraction or depression. If planned savings are more than planned investment, it leads to decline in consumption, price, investment, income and finally reduces the savings.

(ii) If PS<PI, it takes the economy to expansion or prosperity. If planned savings are less than planned investment, it leads to increase in consumption, price, investment, income and finally increases the savings.

(iii) After working out of both the forces, the equilibrium will be restored and savings will become equal to investment, i.e. RS=RI.

Keynes Paradox of Thriftiness

Keynes introduced the 'Paradox of Thrift' to explain how the increase in savings not only reduces the income and other economic activities but also savings itself at the end. Keynes says that saving may be virtue to an individual but when all the people save their income definitely it will be vice to the nation. He further argues that the increase in savings reduces consumption, effective demand, MEC, investments, income and employment and finally the savings. It is illustrated in Fig. 4.6.

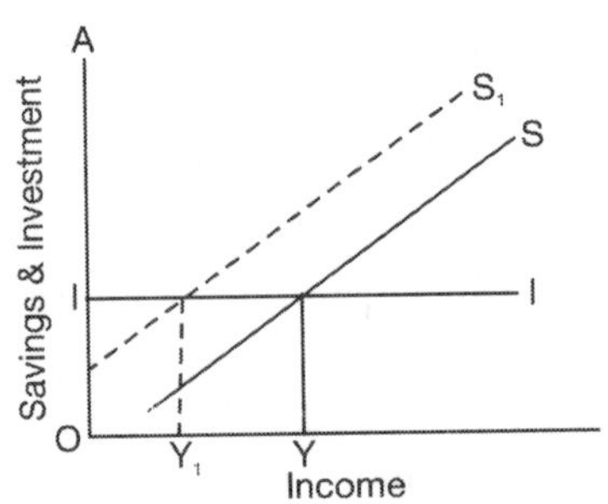

Fig. 4.6: Keynes' Paradox of Thriftiness

S is the original savings curve. I is investment curve.

The increase in savings reduces consumption, investment and eventually income from Y to Y_1 so the savings declines which is by new S_1 curve. It is Keynes' paradox of thriftiness.

4.4 MODEL QUESTIONS

2-Marks Questions

1. What is Acceleration Principle?
2. When capital: output ratio is 100:50, find out the value of v.

3. Name any two assumptions of accelerator.
4. What do you mean by acceleration effect?
5. Find out the value of gross investment when v=2, Y_n= 150 and Y_{n-1}= 100.
6. Give any two limitations of acceleration.
7. What do you mean by leverage-effect?
8. Find out the value of super multiplier when c=0.5 and d=0.2.
9. Mention any two limitations of interaction between k and v.
10. What do you mean by ex-ante savings and investment?

5-Marks Questions

1. Write a note on assumptions of acceleration.
2. When ΔIa=200, c=0.5, d=0.2, find out the value of income propagation.
3. Write a short-note on criticisms on interaction between k and v.
4. Write a note on interaction between k and v.
5. Compare between multiplier and acceleration.
6. Write a note on Keynes' paradox of thrift.

10-Marks Questions

1. Define acceleration principle. Explain its working.
2. What is accelerator? Explain its assumptions and criticisms.
3. What is leverage-effect? Give its mathematical illustration.
4. What is interaction? Explain its limitations and importance.
5. Explain the savings and investment controversy.

5

Business Cycle

5.1. BUSINESS CYCLES

5.1.1 Meaning and Definitions

Business cycle or trade cycle is an important feature of the working of a capitalist economy and such economy is regularly experiencing alternating periods of prosperity and depression. The British economists call it "Trade Cycle". While the American economists prefer to use the term "Business Cycles". But it should be noted that the term trade cycle or business cycle should not be conceived as limited to the fluctuations in the realm of trade of business only. It refers to the entire economic system as a whole.

A business cycle is a very complex economic phenomenon. The economists have not been able so far to find out any comprehensive explanation for this phenomenon. The business cycle is associated with sweeping fluctuations in economic activities such as production, prices, employment, wages, interest profits, income, etc.

Business cycle implies a wave-like fluctuation in aggregate economic activities particularly in national income, employment, wages, prices and output. It occurs in a more or less regular time sequence. It is mostly present in a capitalistic society or market-operated economy. These fluctuations rarely occur in a well-planned socialist economy.

Definitions: Economists have defined business cycle in various ways. Some important definitions are discussed as under:

(i) Prof. W.C. Mitchell defines business cycle as "Business cycles are a species of fluctuations in the economic activities of organized communities...."

(ii) J.M. Keynes defines business cycle as "A trade cycle is composed of periods of good trade characterized by rising prices and low unemployment percentages, altering with periods of bad trade characterized by falling prices and high unemployment percentages".

Keynes has specified two indices, namely prices and unemployment, for measuring the upswing and downswing of the business cycles.

(iii) Frederic Benham gives definition on business cycle as "A trade cycle may be defined rather badly, as a period of prosperity followed by a period of depression. It is not surprising that economic process should be irregular trade being good at some time and bad at others".

(iv) Prof. A.H. Hansen defines trade cycle as "the business cycle is peculiarly a manifestation of the industrial segment of the economy from which prosperity or depression is redistributed to other groups in the highly inter related modern society".

(v) A.C. Pigou has defined trade cycle as "All the recorded cycles are members of the same family, but among them there are no twins".

On the basis of above definitions, business cycles, thus, are rhythmical changes or the cyclical movements in aggregate aspect of the economic activities. In other words, business cycles, therefore, are the fluctuations in income, employment output and prices.

5.1.2 Features

The features of business cycle can be drawn on the basis of the definitions given above. It occurs periodically in wave-like fashion with varying magnitude affecting not only the entire economy of the country but also making its impact on economies of other countries of the world. The following are the some important features of business cycle.

(i) It Occurs Periodically: Business cycle occurs periodically. It means the prosperity and depression will be occurring alternatively. But they need not be uniform in the extent and magnitude. They are not perfectly rhythmical in character.

(ii) It is Universal: Business cycles are universal or all-pervasive in their influence on the national economy as well as the international economy. W.C. Mitchell pointed out that the expansion as well as contraction occur simultaneously in many economic sectors. Moreover, expansion and contraction are transmitted from one country to others through the mechanism of international trade and hence the effects of business cycles are experienced throughout the trading world. Thus, it is international in character. For example, the wordwide Great Depression of 1929.

(iii) It is Wave-like Movement: The business cycle will have a set pattern of movements which is analogous to waves. The rising prices, production, employment and prosperity will become the features of upward movement. The falling prices, employment, income and contraction will become the features of the downward movement.

(iv) The Process is Cumulative and Self-Reinforcing: The upward movement and downward movement are cumulative in their process. Once the upward movement starts, it creates further movement in the same direction by feeding on itself. This momentum will persist till the forces accumulative to alter the direction and create the downward movement. When downward movement starts, it persists in the same direction leading to the worst depression and stagnation till it is retrieved to gain upward movement. Therefore, there cannot be either an indefinite prosperity or an indefinite depression. Sooner or later period of prosperity must come to an end and give way to the depression. Similarly, the period of depression must come to an end sooner or later and pave the way for the prosperity.

(v) The Fluctuations are More in Prices of Agricultural Goods than Industrial Goods: The fluctuations in prices are more in the markets of agricultural products than industrial products. On the other hand, the fluctuations in output and employment are more marked in the industrial sector than in the agricultural sector.

(vi) Business Cycles are Similar but not Identical: The different cycles and waves in the business cycles will be similar in general features. Each business cycle is constructed typically but it is not identical with other in all respects. The typical cycle is not an exact replica of any other individual cycle. The rhythm is rough and imperfect. All the recorded business cycles are members of the same family, about among them there are no twins.

(vii) It is Synchronic in character: The expansion and contraction occur approximately at the same periods in all industries. There is almost a uniform effect of every phase of the cycle on every firm. The economic system is like a human body. The business cycle is like a pin prick that shakes the entire human body. Thus, the phases of the cycle tend to appear in all types of activities but in varying degrees.

(viii) Business Cycles Occur Periodically: Business cycles occur at fairly regular intervals. The period of interval cannot be stated precisely. But the degree of regularity is just sufficient and adequate to indicate the periodicity of a business cycle. It is not possible to earmark exact and uniform duration for the completion of a cycle but the expansion and contraction are sure to follow one another without fail.

(ix) The Trade Cycle is Characterized by the Presence of a Crisis: The trade cycle has the presence of a crisis like the peak or the trough. The peak and the trough are not symmetrical means the downward movement is more sudden and violent than the change from downward to upward. The up-turn is not easily noticeable while the down-turn which is sharp and steep can be easily noticeable.

(x) The Upward and Downward Swings Move Parallel with Economic Activities: The upward and downward swings of a business cycle move parallel with economic activities like production, demand for and supply of money, etc. The Quantity of Money rises during prosperity and falls during depression.

(xi) Business Cycles Differ in Timing and Amplitude: Some business cycles are mild, some others are severe. Some trade cycles are of two to four years duration, some others have the period of eight to ten years or even more. The upward swing in some cycles is longer than the downward swing; on the contrary it is vice versa.

(xii) Business Cycle is a General Macroeconomic Phenomena: Trade cycles affect every segment of the economy. Fluctuations in production, employment, income and prices are not confined to all the segments of the economy. Therefore, they are Macroeconomic in nature.

In addition to these features, the American Economic Association found out the following important features of a business cycle:

(a) Prices and production other than agriculture generally rise or fall together.

(b) Total output and employment fluctuate by a larger percentage in durable and capital goods industries than in non-durable and consumption goods industries.

(c) Large changes in total output, employment and the price level are normally accompanied by large changes in currency, credit and velocity of circulation of money in the same direction.

(d) Prices of manufactured goods are comparatively rigid while prices of agricultural goods are normally flexible.

(e) Profits fluctuate by much larger percentage than other types of income.

(f) Fluctuations in production, employment, and prices are not confined to one or a few industries but extend to all industries. The industries are so interconnected that the wave of prosperity or depression in one industry passes on to the others.

(g) The cyclical fluctuations tend to be not only national but also international in character. Prosperity and depression spreads from one country to another through foreign trade. The trade cycle is thus a world phenomenon.

Thus, the trade cycles are very complex phenomena. They are the result of various exogamous and endogamous factors. Therefore, they vary widely in their duration and intensity.

5.1.3 Phases of Business Cycles

A wave-like fluctuation of economic activities passes different phases before completion of a cycle. A depression to another depression or prosperity to prosperity is called completion of a cycle. Some economists divide a trade cycle into four phases and some other economists divide them into five phases. However, by considering full employment as a phase, a typical or standard business cycle is divided into five phases, namely (i) Depression, (ii) Recovery—Revival, (iii) Full employment, (iv) Prosperity—Boom and (v) Recession. These five phases of the business cycle are illustrated in Fig. 5.1.

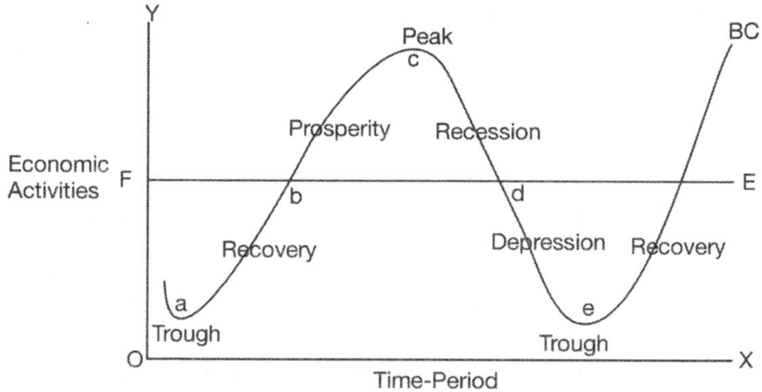

Fig. 5.1: Phases of Business Cycle

In the figure, FE is the full employment line. Above this line, we have two phases of the business cycle—a prosperity (bc) in the upswing and a recession in the downswing (cd). Below this line, again, we have two phases of the business cycle—recovery in the upswing (ab) and depression in the downswing (de). Trough is the bottom of depression and Peak is the top of prosperity. The business cycle as shown in the figure passes through five phases or stages. It starts with depression to be followed by recovery, prosperity, boom, recession and ultimately ends up again with depression. At the end of depression, again recovery or revival starts. Thus, each phase runs its own course and gives way to its succeeding phase. However, the time-interval of any of these phases is not definite.

Since a trade cycle is a continuous phenomenon, it can hardly be said to have any beginning. The phases of a cycle constitute an endless chain of events, one following the other. These phases of a business cycle are discussed as under:

(i) Depression Phase: Depression is the contraction or downswing phase of trade cycle. This constitutes the first phase of a business cycle. During this period, business activities in the country are below the normal state. The depression is characterized by the following features:

(a) The price level is very low.

(b) The volume of production and trade is falling.

(c) Unemployment is very high.

(d) Profit margins do not exist: firms suffer losses.

(e) Wages, interest and rent are all falling to a very low level.

(f) Bank credit contracts and bank clearings are also very low.

(g) Aggregate expenditure and the affective demand go on declining.

(h) There is no opportunity to invest; stock market is dull and stock prices are falling to a low level.

(i) All construction activities come to, more or less, complete standstill during a depression.

(j) There is thus over all pessimism in the economy.

(k) During depression, preference for liquidity increases.

(l) The consumer goods industries are however least affected. But the capital goods industries come to complete standstill.

(m) All sections of the people in the economy suffer: some suffer more than others. For instance, the farmers suffer badly because the prices of agricultural goods fall more rapidly than those of manufactured goods because of the inability of the farmers to adjust their output with the declining demand. The working classes are the worst sufferers in the depression because of falling income and growing unemployment.

The two longest depressions in the USA history were those of 1873-79 (65 months) and 1929-33 (44 months).

However, a depression cannot be regarded as a permanent feature of an economy. In fact, the very forces which cause the depression are themselves self-defeating. For, during a depression, businessmen postpone replacement of their plant and machinery and consumers postpone the purchase of durable goods. Hence, the need for replacement and the purchase of durable goods gradually accumulate.

Hence, after a period of time, there will be a moderate increase in the purchase of durable goods on the consumers' part and replacement of plant and machinery on the part of producers. This will call for an increase in production, in turn leading to an increase in employment, income and aggregate effective demand. Banks will be anxious to expand credit by reducing rate of interest. Gradually, pessimism vanishes and optimism develops and economic activities once again gather momentum. Thus, a stage of recovery sets in.

(ii) Revival Phase or Recovery: The revival or recovery phase refers the lower turning point at which an economy undergoes change from depression to prosperity. With an improvement in demand for capital goods, recovery sets in. When the demand for consumption goods rises or when the capital stock increases, the demand for capital goods will rise and new investment will be induced. Such induced investment will cause a rise in employment and income. The increased income in turn will lead to a rise in consumption which will push up the demand further which in turn leads to a rise in prices, profits, further investment, employment and income. The increased income in turn will lead to a rise in consumption which will push up the demand further which in turns leads to a rise in prices, profits, further investment, employment and income. Once the expansionary movement starts, that is how it gathers momentum. The revival phase is characterized by the following features:

(a) The level of prices, production, employment and income slowly and steadily rises.

(b) The stock market becomes more sensitive.

(c) The rise in stock prices will favour expansion and speed up the revival.

(d) The expectations of the businessmen will improve and optimism develops in the business community.

(e) The profit-margin which had fallen extremely low during depression slowly rises.

(f) Bank-loans and demand for credit start rising. Bank-reserves slowly decline and bank-clearings increase along with the revival of business and investment.

g) The expectations of the entrepreneurs improve and business optimism leads to the stimulation of development investment.

(h) With the recovery in industrial sector, the agricultural sector of the economy also recovers.

(i) Through multiplier and acceleration effects, the economy proceeds upwards steadily and rapidly.

(j) The process of recovery becomes cumulative. Increased business and factor income result in increased expenditure which causes further increase in income and business activity which in turn result in further increased expenditure and so on.

The wave of recovery, once initiated, begins to feed upon itself. The rate of recovery has a direct relationship with the rate of preceding depression. The more severe the depression, the more rapid will be the recovery. It is difficult say the definiteness regarding the duration of the recovery phase. It depends upon the forces which initiate the recovery. The recovery phase may be initiated by new innovations, government expenditure changes in the techniques of production, investment in new regions, etc.

(iii) Full Employment Phase: The cumulative process of recovery or revival continues till the economy reaches the stage of full employment. Full employment implies that all the available resources in men and materials are fully employed. During this phase, the level of economic activity is optimum and all the factors of production are fully employed. There is no involuntary unemployment. However, there may be a small percentage of voluntary and frictional unemployment but unemployment of such types is compatible with the notion of full employment. The full employment phase is characterized by the following features:

(a) There is an all-round stability of economic values like output, wage, price and income.

(b) Rent, wages, interest and profits are high.

(c) Output is the highest under given technology.

(d) Employment is at maximum level and unemployment is at lowest level.

(e) Trade and commerce are extensive.

(f) Bank credit and bank clearing are large.

(g) Business failures are very few.

(h) There is heavy investment in capital goods' industries.

(i) Business confidence is at its highest.

(j) A high rate of formation of new business enterprises and full employment.

(k) There is a general feeling of optimism among businessmen and industrialists.

(iv) Prosperity: The stage of full employment follows by the stage of economic prosperity. According to Haberler, prosperity is "a state of affairs in which the real income consumed, real income produced and level of employment are high or rising and there are no idle resources or unemployed workers or very few of either". The phase of prosperity is characterized by a number of features such as

(a) Increased production and trade.

(b) High level of income and employment.

(c) High level of effective demand.

(d) High marginal efficiency of capital.

(e) High capital investment in basic industries.

(f) High prices.

(g) High profits.

(h) High rate of formation of new business enterprises.

(i) Full employment of resources.

(j) General feeling of optimism among industrialists and businessmen.

The longest sustained period of prosperity occurred in the USA during 1923 to 1929 with some minor interruptions in 1924.

The prosperity phase also consists of inflation or boom. It paves the way for the rise of boom or inflation. The continuance of investment even after the stage of full employment results in a sharp inflationary rise of prices. This causes undue optimism among businessmen and industrials that make additional investments in the various branches of the economy. This puts additional pressure on the factors of production which are already fully employed, causing a sharp rise in their prices. Soon a situation develops in which the number of jobs exceeds the number of workers available in the market such a situation is known as over full employment. Profits touch a new high. Attracted by the rising profits, the industrialists and businessmen further increase their capital investments. This adds fuel to the fire. Run away or galloping inflation raises its head in all its ugliness. Prices rise sky-high. The tempo of the boom reaches new heights, i.e. peak. There is an atmosphere of over optimism all around.

But the developing boom carries with it the seeds of self-destruction. Bottlenecks begin to appear in the various sectors of the economy. Factors of production become scarce, causing further spurt in their prices. The cost of calculations of the businessmen and the industrialists are completely upset. Some new hastily set-up firms collapse. This makes the businessmen over cautious. They now begin to stay away from new projects and even stop the expansion of the existing business units. It prepares the ground for the succeeding stage. A boom, as it is said, is inevitably followed by a bust that is recession sets in.

(v) Recession: When prosperity ends, recession begins. Recession refers to the upper turning point when the economy experiences a turn from prosperity to depression. Recessionary phase lasts for a relatively shorter period of time. During recession, the forces of expansion are over powered by the forces of contraction.

Recession marks the upper turning point of a business cycle. From the upper turning point onwards the forces which lead to expansion of business activities gain the forces of contraction. The recession sets in because of the following reasons:

(a) Increased bottlenecks, or critical shortages of raw materials, skilled labour and management.

(b) Increased strength of trade unions leading to pressures for increased wages and improved working conditions.

(c) Tightened conditions in money market and capital market and rising interest rates.

(d) Miscalculations of entrepreneurs.

(e) Over-optimism is replaced by over-pessimism.

Due to the effects of the above forces bottlenecks begin to appear in the various sectors of the economy. Factors of production, particularly, raw materials and labour force become scarce and command higher prices and wages continuously. The cost of production, therefore, goes up very high and upsets the calculations of the entrepreneurs. The businessmen realize their mistakes and find that many of the ventures started in the rosy anticipation of the boom are not profitable. This trend in their thinking has cumulative effects. The feeling of over-optimism of his boom period is replaced by over-pessimism characterized by fear, doubt and hesitation. Not only are the new projects postponed for some remote future date but even those in hands are abandoned. Credit is suddenly curtailed sharply by the banks as they are afraid of failures. Business expansion stops. Orders are cancelled out and workers are laid off. Failure of business units increases investment ceases and unemployment rises. There is a landslide in prices and confidence of the businessmen is rudely shaken. Liquidity preference suddenly increases and people prefer to hold cash rather than invest in business.

Construction activity shows down and unemployment appears in construction industries. Unemployment spreads to the other sectors of the economy, because the multiplier begins to work in the downward direction. Unemployment leads to a fall in incomes, expenditure, prices, profits and industrial and trade activities. There is panic in the stock market and prices of stocks and shares fall rapidly. As business activity declines, bank clearing drop down while bank reserves pile up due to the withdrawal of old loans and refusal of fresh loans. A feeling of terror which paralyses and converts retreat into advance prevails all over the economy. The rate of interest rises at the same time to make confusion worst confounded. Once the business and economic activities start declining, it becomes highly impossible to stop it. It ends in a hopeless depression. Thus, a business cycle completes.

5.1.4 Types of Business Cycles

Every business cycle differs from other in various respects like period, amplitude, etc. On the basis of the length of the phases of the business cycle, Professor James Arthur Estey has classified the trade cycles as (i) Major Cycles, (ii) Minor Cycles, (iii) Building cycles (iv) Kondratieff Cycles and (v) Long Waves.

(i) Major Cycles: According to Hansen, major business cycles have an average length ranging from six to thirteen years. Prof. Hansen recognizes twelve major business cycles in the USA during the period from 1837 to 1937, with an average duration of 8.33 years and ten major business cycles with an average duration of eight years between 1857 and 1937.

According to American economists, Major business cycles are the economic fluctuations between major recessions. The recession of 1929 was a major one and therefore, the business cycle that followed it was a major cycle.

When British or European economists speak of 'business cycles' or trade cycles they refer to such major cycles. A major cycle is a cycle occurring in the interval between major recessions of economic activities. Usually, it is measured from one trough (lower turning point) to the next trough. A major business cycle is characterized by the fluctuations in output, employment, prices over a relatively longer period of six to thirteen years.

The major trade cycles are sometimes referred to as 'Juglar Cycle', after the name of Clement Juglar, a French economist of the nineteenth century, who, on the basis of his investigation, established the cyclical nature of business fluctuations.

It has been established from the records of business fluctuations that each major cycle is made up of two or three minor cycles. The upswing of business in the major cycle is often interrupted by minor down swings. Likewise, the downswings of business in the major cycle may be interrupted by minor upswings. These shorter cycles in major cycles are sometimes referred to as minor cycles.

After Juglar other economists worthy of mention, who made detailed study of the problem, were Joseph Kitchen and Russian economist Nikolai D. Kondratieff. Kitchen's thesis that business cycles were of two varieties, namely major cycles and minor cycles was based on the data relating to interest rates, bank clearing, and whole sale prices in England and USA. The duration of the major cycle ranged between six years and ten years.

From the economic policy point of view, the major cycles are of greater importance. Sometimes, minor cycles may go unnoticed whereas the major business cycles have got serious impact on the economy. But at the same time major cycles have greater impact on international level. According to James Arthur Estey, "Major cycles are dramatic and have serious results".

(ii) Minor Cycles: Minor cycles are cycles in which the length varies from three to five years. Minor cycles do not have serious effects on output, employment and prices. Ups and downs of economic activities in minor cycles are like oscillations on either side of the equilibrium position. Minor cycles are usually interruptions in major upswings and downswings of business activities. Minor cycles are associated normally with changes in inventory investment based on short-term expectations of businessmen. On the other hand, major cycles are associated with large changes in the rate of real net investment based on long-term expectations of business units. Minor cycles are also known as Kitchen cycles after Joseph Kitchen who first distinguished minor cycles in his studies of cyclical fluctuations.

As per the records of business fluctuations, each major cycle is made up of two or three minor cycles.

The upswing of business in the major cycle is often interrupted by minor downswings. Likewise the downswings of business in the major cycle may be interrupted by minor upswing. These shorter cycles in major cycles are sometimes referred to as minor cycles. The duration of the minor cycles averages close to 40 months. These minor cycles have actually operated both in UK and the USA.

According to A.H. Hansen, economic fluctuations that may be termed as minor cycles range in length, measured from trough to trough, from a minimum of two years to a maximum of five years. The length of three years seems to be a model figure. A.H. Hansen has made a study of 73 year period (1865-1938) and on the basis of his study has concluded that there were altogether 18 cycles in the USA during this 73 year period the eleven were minor cycles. As per Alvin Hansen, study report during the period 1857-1937, their occurred in the USA 23 minor cycles with an average duration of 3.48 years.

As per the study reports of eminent economists of UK and the USA, major and minor cycles both are found in the economic fluctuations between major recessions. For instance, the recession of 1929 was a major one and therefore the cycle that followed it was a major cycle. No doubt major cycles are more important in framing the economic policies sometimes minor cycles may go unnoticed, whereas the major cycles have got serious impact on the economy. According to J.A. Estey, "minor oscillations (cycles) are not dramatic, they may scarcely be recognized as they go by...."

(iii) Building Cycles: Building cycles refer to the cycle of building construction business. The building cycles have their expansion and contraction and have longer duration than the Juglar cycles. It has been discovered that the building industry is also subject to fluctuations of a fairly regular duration. The duration of building cycle varies between fifteen to twenty years. The average duration of building cycles is of eighteen years. It is just twice the length of the business cycles. Between 1830 and 1934, there were six complex building cycle in the USA. Between 1933-34 and 1944-45 a short building cycle of eleven years occurred. It means that there are two types of building cycles: (a) Long building cycles and (b) Short building cycles. For instance, the outbreak of war in 1914 interrupted the normal course of a trade cycle. The cycle which had nearly reached its peak in 1913 would have, in normal course, taken a downward turn either in

1914 or 1915. The outbreak of the World War I in 1914, however, stretched forward the upper limb of the trade cycle.

Similarly, the outbreak of World War II in 1939 interrupted the normal course of the cycle which had reached its peak in the summer of 1937. The rearmament programme occasioned by war turned the decline which had then just begun into a swift recovery. Further the wavelength is not uniform and similar in every sector of the economy. It is interesting to note that fluctuations in building construction industries have an average length of almost twice the length of the normal business cycle.

(iv) Kondratieff Cycles: Russian economist Kondratieff had discovered some trade cycles hence they were called Kondratieff cycles. They are long waves. Kondratieff, on the basis of statistical data pertaining to the period 1780-1920, was able to establish 2½ long cycles in England and France each full cycle being of the duration of 60 years. Kondratieff had suggested in 1925 the possibility of the existence of longer cycles with average duration approximating 50 years. These long cycles in Kondratieff opinion were international in scope and were caused by the same dynamic forces which caused the regular intermediate-length cycles of 7-10 years duration.

J.A. Schumpeter in his studies of business cycles occurred in England and France found out (i) the upward movement of the first cycle (1789-1814) was due to the Industrial Revolution (ii) the upward movement of the second cycle (1814-96) was due to the use of steam and steel and (iii) the upward movement of the third cycle (1896-1920) was due to discovery of electricity, the development of chemistry and the use of motors. Such major waves of innovations will cause the long business cycles. These innovations produced profound and prolonged effects on economic progress. This marked the beginning of the upswing (caused by innovations) of a long wave cycles.

(v) Long Waves: Long waves' fluctuations have occurred in 'wholesale prices'. General prices have changed their direction five times between 1790 and 1930—roughly a period of 140 years. Such long wave fluctuations have occurred both in the USA and UK. These fluctuations (cycles) in prices are because of the fluctuations in the supply gold compared to the level of production. Therefore, the writers like J.A. Estey expressed their doubt about whether these long wave fluctuations can be called as 'true cycle' or not. However, the fluctuations in the general level of prices are accompanied by the fluctuations in the general level of economic activities. Long wave fluctuations of 50 to 60 years have taken place.

5.2 BUSINESS CYCLES THEORIES

Causes for happening of trade cycles are the major dispute among the economists. The economists have developed the various theories from time to time to explain the causes for occurring of trade cycles, their periodicity and synchronism. They are:

(i) The Climatic Theory or Jevons's Sun-Spot Theory: The periodical appearance of sun-spots brings changes in economic activities through changes in harvests in agriculture.

(ii) Psychological Theory: Business activities are mainly organized by intelligent business people and their anticipations always influence on business activities. Their optimism and pessimism psychological waves would influence and create fluctuations in business activities.

(iii) Overproduction Theory: The competitions among the firms create overproduction in free capitalist economy. The over-production creates disequilibrium in the economy which leads to ups and downs in economic activities.

(iv) Over-savings or Under-consumption Theory: J.A. Hobson and Major Douglas, socialists, argued that the disparities in distribution of income between rich and poor lead to over-savings or under-consumption in the economy. It is because the rich people save more who have more income and poor people spend less on consumption who receive less income. So it creates ups and downs in economic activities in the economy.

(v) Hayek's Theory: According to Hayek, the ups and downs in business activities take place in the economy due to change in banks' credit policy. The over-issue of credit leads to expansion and under-issue of credit leads to contraction.

(vi) J.R. Hicks' Theory: Hicks used acceleration principle of co-efficient to explain the ups and downs in economic activities through the influence of investment on income. Prof. Harrod, R. Frisch and P. Samuelson too used this to explain the nature and types of trade cycles occur in the economy.

(vii) The Cobweb Theorem: Nicholas Kaldor (first time 1934), Umberto Ricci (Italy), Schultz (Holland) and Tinbergen (USA) propounded this theory to explain the causes of trade cycle. The theory explains that the action and reaction of price, production, demand and supply in current and subsequent periods would create ups and downs in economic activities in the economy.

(viii) Monetary Theory: R.G. Hawtrey has propounded this theory and he explains that the variations in flows of money through banking system create ups and downs in economic activities in the economy.

(ix) Keynes' Savings and Investment Theory: According to J.M. Keynes, the disequilibrium between savings and investment creates ups and downs in economic activities in the economy.

(x) J.A. Schumpeter's Innovation Theory: He has explained the business cycle in terms of innovations that take place in the economic system of a capitalist country from time to time.

By taking into account the kernels of all the theories on trade cycle the various causes of trade cycle are grouped into three heads as: (a) unforeseen causes affecting the supply of raw materials; (b) imperfect adjustments of demand and supply and (c) variations in prices due to financial causes.

5.2.1 Hawtrey's Pure Monetary Theory

Hawtrey's pure monetary theory of trade cycle can be discussed in details as under:

Central Idea

This theory of business cycles is mainly developed by Prof. R.G. Hawtrey, an English economist who enjoys the reputation of adhering most uncompromisingly to a purely monetary explanation of business cycles. He says "The trade cycle is a purely monetary phenomenon because general demand is itself a monetary phenomenon".

He argued that all the changes in economic activities are nothing but reflections of changes in the flow of money. Thus, he holds firmly to the view that the causes of cyclical fluctuations were to be found only in those factors that produce expansions and contractions in the flow of money—money supply. Hence, the ultimate cause of economic fluctuations lies in the monetary system.

According to Prof. R.G. Hawtrey, the main factor affecting the flow of money, i.e. money supply, is the credit creation by the banking system. He further argued that the changes in income and expenditure are caused by changes in the volume of bank credit. The real causes of the business cycle can be traced to variations in effective demand which occurred due to changes in bank credit. He points out that it is the rate of progress of bank credit development that determines the extent and duration of the cycle, thus he said "when credit movements are accelerated, the period of the cycle is shortened". It implies that if credit facilities do not exist, the fluctuation will not occur. Therefore, by controlling credit, one can control fluctuations in the economic activity.

Prof. R.G. Hawtrey further maintains that although the rate progress of cycles may be influenced by non-monetary causes, these factors operate indirectly and through the medium of the credit movement. For instance, a non-monetary factor such as optimism in a particular industry can affect activity directly, but it cannot exert a general influence on industry unless optimism is allowed to reflect itself through monetary changes, i.e. through increased borrowing. On these grounds Prof. R.G. Hawtrey regarding trade cycle as a purely monetary phenomenon.

The gist of Prof. Hawtrey's theory is that the inherent instability in bank credit causes changes in the flow of money which in effect leads to cyclical variations. In economic activities, an economic expansion is caused by the expansion of bank credit and economic crisis will occur as soon as the credit creation is stopped by the banking system, thus a contraction of credit leads to a depression.

Properties of the Theory

R.G. Hawtrey's theory is based on the following postulates:

(i) The consumers' income is the aggregate of money income = national income or community's income in general.

(ii) The consumers' outlay is the aggregate of money spending on consumption and investment.

(iii) The consumers' total outlay constitutes community's aggregate effective demand for real goods and services. Thus, general demand is a monetary demand.

(iv) The wholesalers or traders have strategic position in the economy. They are extremely sensitive in their stock hoarding business to the changes in the rate of interest.

(v) The changes in the flow of money are usually caused by the unstable nature of bank credit.

According to Prof. R.G. Hawtrey, the changes in business activity are due to variations in consumers' outlay or effective demand. It is the total money income that determines consumers' outlay. The stability of the whole economic system follows from the establishment of monetary equilibrium.

Assumptions

Hawtrey's theory is based on the following assumptions.

(a) Consumers' outlay must be equal to consumers' income.

(b) Consumption should be equal to production.

(c) Cash balances of consumers and traders should remain unchanged.

(d) Bank credit flow must be steady.

(e) Market rate of interest should be equal to the profit rate.

(f) Wages and prices on the whole are equal.

(g) There is no net export or import of gold.

Prof. Hawtrey contends that these assumptions are necessary to attain monetary equilibrium situation which is one of the extremely delicate balances that can be easily disclosed by any number of causes and when disturbed tends to move into a transitional period of cumulative disequilibrium. He emphasized that primarily it is unstable nature of the credit system in the economy that causes changes in the flow of money and disturbs the monetary equilibrium. In this connection, he feels that the discount rate or interest rate exerts a great influence.

Explanation

Hawtrey's theory on trade cycle can be explained with reference the each swing of the cycle.

(A) **Revival and Up-Swing:** According to Prof. R.G. Hawtrey, the expansion phase of the trade cycle is brought about by an increase of bank credit and lasts so long as the credit expansion goes on. A credit expansion is brought about by banks through the easing lending conditions along with a reduction in the discount rate or interest rate, thereby reducing the costs of credit.

Banks stimulate borrowing by lowering their lending rates. Such a reduction in the interest rate is a great stimulus to traders or borrowers. According to Hawtrey, traders are in a strategic position as they tend to carry their large stocks primarily with borrowed money. Moreover, traders usually mark their profits as fraction of the value of a large turnover of goods. Hence, a small change in the interest rate affects their profits to a disproportionately large extent. Thus, they are very sensitive to change in the rate of interest.

Trades are induced to increase their stocks-inventories, when the interest rate falls. Hence, they give large order to the producers; the increased order of traders causes the producers to raise their level of production and employment. This in turn leads to an increase in income and monetary demand. "Thus the whole amount of the funds created by the bank is received as income whether profits, wages, rents, salaries, or interest, by those engaged in producing the commodities." Evidently, the increased production leads to an expansion of consumers' income and outlay. Further to meet increased consumers' demand the producers undertake productive activities that once again results into further rise in consumers' income, outlay and demand. This process continues. This process leads to a cumulative expansion which is being propelled by the continuous expansion of bank credit.

Hawtrey further states that "productive activity cannot grow without limit. As the cumulative process carries one industry after another to the limit of productive capacity procedures begin to quote higher and higher prices". Thus, when prices rise, traders have a further incentive to borrow and hold more stocks in view of the rising profits. The rising prices operate in the same way as falling interest rates and the spiral of cumulative expansion is accelerated further. This means that there are three important factors which influence credit expansion by banks. These are: (a) The rate of interest charged by the banks, (b) Traders' expectations about the price behaviour and (c) The actual magnitude of their sales.

The rate of interest is determined by the banks. Traders' expectations depend on general business conditions and their psychology. Actual magnitude of sales depends on the net effect of the consumer's outlay. In brief, optimism encourages borrowing, borrowing accelerates sales, and sales accelerate optimism. A cumulative process upwards begins with increased income, employment and output.

(B) **The Crisis and Down-Swing:** Hawtrey argues that the prosperity comes to an end when credit expansion ends. As banks go on increasing credit, their cash funds deplete and they are forced to curtail credit and raise interest rates in order to discourage the demand for new loans. The rise in the interest rates causes the bubble to burst. The upward swing characterized by rising prices and higher incomes gives place to the downward swing characterized by falling incomes and low level of economic activities. The sudden suspension of credit facilities by banks comes as a bolt from the blue to the businessmen. It is because they were enjoying the liberal credit policy of the banks for the expansion of their business. But now contrary to their expectations, they receive notices from the banks to pay back their loans. In order to meet the sudden calls from banks, they try to dispose of their stocks as quickly as possible at any price and repay the loans. The eagerness on the part of the businessmen to dispose of their stock will definitely depress the market and bring down the prices as well as profits. With every fall in the prices of goods and profits of the businessmen, their eagerness to dispose of the stocks as quickly as possible will lead to confusion and collapse of the market. Marginal and average firms may go for liquidation of their production-stock. This worsens the situation in the market still further and makes the banks extremely nervous. Therefore, the banks adopt still more restrictive measures to reduce their credit. Thus, with every fall in the bank credit, prices, production, employment, income consumer outlays or effective demand, etc. will also go on falling continuously. Thus, the process of contraction sets in and like the process of expansion become cumulative. The contraction spirals in a downward direction continues till it reaches the lowest possible level. The downward movement in the economy sets in and ultimately gives place to the downswing of the trade cycle.

The process of contraction, like the process of expansion, cannot also be permanent. When the economy is working at a very low level, the banking community, because of the excess cash reserves, decides to adopt a liberal credit policy to expand credit. They therefore lower the rate of interest to induce businessmen to borrow and expand their business. This brings about a revival and the period of revival is ready followed by prosperity of revival and boom.

In brief, according to Hawtrey, "The trade cycle is nothing but a small scale replica of an out-right money inflation and deflation". In other words, the trade cycle is due to variations in the volume of money and credit. Thus, he said that the inherently unstable nature of the modern monetary and credit system is the mother of fluctuations in the economic activities. Further he argues that an intelligent bank policy designed to maintain stability of the price level would not merely reduce but also abolish trade cycles. Hawtrey concludes that the main cause for the business cycle is the commercial banking system and therefore it is called 'business cycle a purely monetary phenomenon'.

Criticisms

Hawtrey's theory has been supported by many economists like Milton Friedman and Clark Warburton, the noted American economists. Finance is the life blood of commerce and trade in the modern times. The banking system plays a very significant role in financing economic activities. Nobody can deny that an increase in the volume of money and credit will bring about an expansion of activity and vice versa. However, the critics said like monetary factors there are non-monetary factors which also generate ups and downs in economic activities.

Hawtrey's theory though logically correct, it has been suffering from some shortcomings so it is criticized as under:

(i) Trade Cycle is not a Purely Monetary Phenomenon: Prof. Hawtrey's basic argument is that the trade cycle is a purely monetary phenomenon. But critics did not accept it because according to them the Hawtrey's monetary theory offers an explanation of one important class of economic disorders and it can be corrected by credit-supply management but it does not mean that a community perfectly free from monetary fluctuations would have no economic disorders at all. It leads us to the conclusion that money supply is not the sole and sufficient cause of economics instability.

(ii) It Exaggerated the Role of Wholesalers: According to critics, Prof. R.G. Hawtrey has unnecessarily exaggerated the importance of wholesalers; it was probably because they occupied a strategic position in pre-1914 Great Britain. But now their importance has greatly diminished. Moreover, now a large part of the business financing is done by traders with their own funds rather than by bank credit.

(iii) There is Over-exaggeration of Sensitiveness of Wholesalers to Changes in Interest rate: Prof. Hamberg has raised the objection to Hawtrey's assumption that wholesalers are very sensitive to changes in the rate of interest. He said that the investors may not be more sensitive to change in interest rate because (a) they have their own funds for investment and re-investment activities; (b) they need no or little fund when their sales are unchanged; (c) they may consider the change in interest rate is temporary; and (d) the changes in expectations like price changes, cost of storage, etc. are more important than change in interest rate.

(iv) It is Old Commercial Banking Theory: Prof. R.G. Hawtrey developed his theory on the idea of the old commercial banking school theory, i.e. 'inherent instability of credit' which assumed that the asset-portfolio of banks is heavily loaded with short-term commercial papers. But according to critics in recent times the banking system is much more stable because the banks today hold over 60 per cent of their assets in the form of government securities and the government reacts to expansion and recession in a much different way than the traders do.

(v) It has Undue Faith in Cheap Money Policy: Prof. Hawtrey's believed much in cheap money policy that it helps the continuation prosperity and checks the recession. But Haberler criticized it because when the traders and producers realize that adequate profits are not available to them even the low rate of interest cannot prevent them from reducing their business activities so it sets in recession and depression.

(vi) The Rise in Interest Rate is not the Cause of Crisis: Hawtrey believed that upper turning point is brought about by a rise in the rate of interest which results into crisis or recession. But critics said that the banks raise interest rate because of fund-crisis so the rise in rate of interest is the consequence of crisis. Thus, a rise in interest rate is not actually the cause, but a consequence of the crisis or recession.

(vii) The Theory Neglected the Effect of Expectations: The monetary theory taken into account only monetary factors but it neglected that expectations regarding profit, price, etc. also causes ups and downs in business activities.

(viii) The Theory has no Practical Significance: The lowering the rate of interest during 1930s depression period failed to recover the UK economy from depression so Hawtrey too admitted this failure.

(ix) There is no Explanation about Periodicity: The theory does not give any precise explanation about the periodicity of the cycle.

(x) It is an Incomplete Theory: Myron Ross criticized Hawtrey's theory as an incomplete monetary theory because it has considered only bank credit as monetary factor responsible for trade cycle but it has neglected non-monetary factors like multiplier-accelerator interaction, innovation, rate of profits and the stock of capital which are also responsible for trade cycle.

(xi) It Ignored the Role of Capital Goods Industries: Hawtrey exaggerates the importance of wholesalers, supply of money, and interest rate in his theory. But at the same time, he ignores the role of capital goods industries and other sectors of the economy which also create ups and downs in economic activities.

In brief, it is not correct to say that business fluctuations are caused by the banking system only. The expansion or contraction of bank credit does not cause either boom or depression but once the boom or the depression takes place, the expansion or the contraction of bank credit serves to accentuate it.

5.2.2 Keynes' Trade Cycle Theory

J.M. Keynes has not propounded any theory on trade cycle separately but his theory on income and employment is enough to explain the oscillations in economic activities. In his book *The General Theory of Employment, Interest and Money*, Keynes has given the analysis on trade cycle and its phases.

Keynes has argued that since the rate of interest is stable, the variations in marginal efficiency of capital (MEC) would lead to variations in investment activities which create business cycles.

According to Keynes, investment depends upon interest-rate and marginal efficiency of capital (MEC) so its functional relation is written as: I = (r, MEC). To him, rate of interest could not play so important role in trade cycle and similarly marginal propensity to consume (MPC) also could remain comparatively stable.

Keynes has explained in his income and employment theory that the effective demand consists of both demand for consumers' goods and demand for capital goods and it determines the level of income and employment in the capitalist economy. In short-run consumption function, more or less, remains stable as its determinants are unchangeable. The determinants of investment function are rate of interest and marginal efficiency of capital but the rate of interest remains stable in short-run as the bank lending policies and central bank policy remain unchanged.

Hence, the marginal efficiency of capital plays vital role in income and employment determination. The marginal efficiency of capital is influence by the business expectations that are govern by optimism and pessimism waves. So the variations in marginal efficiency of capital (MEC) would create ups and downs in economic activities or trade cycle in the economy. Keynes' this explanation is called trade cycle theory. It is illustrated in the following chart.

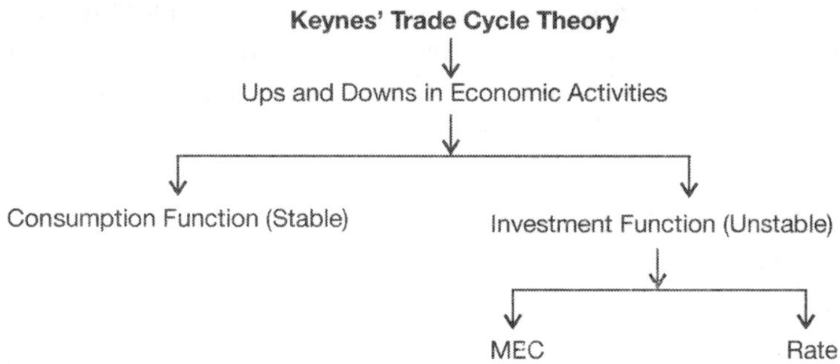

The theory explains the different phases of trade cycle as under:

(i) Revival and Expansion Phases: When the investors expect the higher rate of returns on investment, more investments will take place in the economy thus it leads to revival and expansion of economic activities. The investment multiplier works successfully that leads to increase in income, consumption, output, etc. activities and helps to occur revival and expansion phases.

(ii) Recession and Contraction or Depression Phases: The optimism waves are always followed by the pessimism waves. The increase in investment ultimately leads to decline in profit or rate of return due to increase in cost of production and decrease in price of goods. It takes the economy towards recession and depression.

Neither depression nor expansion remains continuously for long time in the economy. Depression follows recession; recession follows expansion or boom; expansion follows revival and revival follows depression, thus the trade cycle continues further.

Main Points of Keynes' Theory

(i) The variations in investments are responsible for occurring of trade cycles.

(ii) The ups and downs in marginal efficiency of capital lead to variations in investments.

(iii) The business expectations govern the marginal efficiency of capital.

Criticisms

Keynes' trade cycle theory has also certain shortcomings so it is criticized as under:

(i) According to J.A. Estey, Keynes' trade cycle theory is very close to the 'under-consumption theory of trade cycle' so it is not pleading any new thought on trade cycle.

(ii) Robert Gordon criticized the Keynes' trade cycle theory saying that it gave more importance to psychological factors, viz. optimism and pessimism so it is a psychological theory. In reality, the real factors like productivity, resources, technology, etc. also create ups and downs in economic activities thus theory fails to speak full truth.

(iii) Prof. Dudley Dillard criticized Keynes' trade cycle theory saying that the theory explains too more and too less.

(iv) Keynes' theory is not an independent theory to explain the trade cycle: it explains the trade cycle through the income and employment theory.

(v) The theory does not through light on periodicity.

However, the fact cannot be denied that the variations in investments create ups and downs in economic activities.

5.2.3 J.A. Schumpeter's Innovation Theory

Joseph Schumpeter of USA propounded the theory on trade cycled 'innovation theory'. According to him, the innovations are the causes of occurring of trade cycle in the economy. Schumpeter argued that the free capitalist economy has stationary state and it expands and contracts through automatic-adjustment.

There are neither new investments nor net savings in such economy. The current capital formation would be preserved through depreciations. Such economic stability will be destabilized by the innovations. Schumpeter puts it as "The booms consist in the carrying out of innovations in the industrial and commercial organism. By innovations I understand such changes of the combinations of the factors of production as cannot be affected by infinitesimal steps of variations on the margin. They consist primarily in changes in methods of production and transportation, or in changes in industrial organization, or in the production of a new article, or in the opening of new markets or of new sources of material. The recurring periods of prosperity of the cyclical movements are the form progress takes in capitalist society".

He has explained the business cycle in terms of innovations that take place in the economic system of a capitalist country from time to time. By innovation he means the introduction of something new that changes the existing method of production. The innovations may be of following five types:

(a) The introduction of a new product.
(b) The introduction of a new technique of production.
(c) The development of new markets.
(d) The development of new sources of raw-material.
(e) The introduction of changes in the forms of business organization.

Innovation, however, does not arise spontaneously. It must be actively promoted by some agency in the economic system. Such an agent, according to Schumpeter, is an "entrepreneur", entrepreneurs are innovators.

He gives three main reasons for the cluster effect in the appearance of innovations. They are: (a) the social opposition to innovation, (b) the banking system may be unwilling to finance new ideas and projects, and (c) the difficulties in training workers about new techniques.

So long these barriers exist; the process of innovations is greatly slowed down. But as soon as these barriers are lifted, there will be clusters of innovations involving a burst of investment activity. Thus, innovations are essentially non-periodic, discontinuous and bring about the wave-like movements in investment, production, employment, and income. Thus, according to Schumpeter, the innovations create trade cycles in the economy.

The Up-Swing and Prosperity

According to Schumpeter, whenever an innovation takes place in the economy it causes disequilibrium in the existing economic system. This disequilibrium in the economic system continues till there is readjustment at some new equilibrium position.

To explain the upswing and prosperity, Schumpeter assumes that the economy is in a state of full employment and all the productive factors are already fully employed and there is no unemployment.

When innovation takes place in such a society, the equilibrium will be disturbed. The innovations will encourage the investors to place their demand for new techniques and units. They borrow fund from the banks. The banks will create credit that will lead to revival and further revival will be followed by prosperity.

The Down-Swing and Contraction

According to Schumpeter, the prosperity cannot live long because all the firms will come to know the innovations thus it will create competitions among the firms. The competition will lead to overproduction and continuous decline in price and profits. The firms will move to repay bank debts. So the recession sets in and further it will be followed by depression, downswing and contraction.

Further Schumpeter argued that the trade cycles of different lengths occur simultaneously reacting upon one another. Although these different length cycles are caused by one and the same cause, namely innovations, the difference in their lengths is due to the fact that "the periods of gestation and of absorption of effects by the economic system will not, in general, be equal for all the innovations that are undertaken at any time".

Criticisms

Like other trade cycle theories, the innovation theory also suffers from weaknesses. So the following are some important criticisms:

(i) It is Based on Assumption of Full Employment: The assumption of full employment is unrealistic. So the theory fails to give complete explanation of trade cycle.

(ii) The Theory Assumes that Every Innovation in Business is Financed through Expansion of Bank Credit: It is also unrealistic assumption because the innovations in business are mostly financed the development reserves specially kept for the purpose. Thus, business innovations may not cause inflationary pressures in the economy.

(iii) The Innovations are not Sufficient Conditions: Prof. Hayek has stated that innovations alone fail to explain cyclical fluctuation. It is the monetary variations which along with innovations usher in fluctuations in the system. If the entrepreneurs decide to finance innovations with their retained funds, the innovations can generate only mild expansion. Similarly, if the entrepreneurs relay upon the real savings for financing innovations, the inflationary pressures generated by bank credit, will not be felt and the expansion, to a large extent, will be less intense.

(iv) The Theory Greatly Emphasizes on the Entrepreneur: Schumpeter has given greater emphasis to the entrepreneur or the innovator. The process of economic change may be the result of many socio-economic factors. Prof. Hamberg rightly comments as "placing so much importance on the role of the entrepreneur result in too great a role for the element of chance in the path of technological progress, history is the net product of great, underlying socio-economic force".

(v) It Fails to Consider the Competitive Impact of Innovations: The theory fails to the nature of the competitive impact of innovations on the magnitude of trade cycle. If the impact of demand for the new product is widespread reflected in the small decrease in the demand for all other production in general, the loss of demand felt by each one of the old industry will be comparatively mild and readjustment will be easily accomplished.

(vi) Trade Cycle is not a Single Factor Phenomenon: Again critics point out that Schumpeter attributes business cycles, to be phenomenon of innovations only. But the business cycles being a complex phenomenon cannot be attributed to a single factor only.

Despite these shortcomings, Schumpeter treatment is quite fascinating because it attempts to treat cycles in relation to economic growth. Moreover, it combines the endogenous and exogenous business cycle factors in a commendable way.

5.3 MEASURES TO CONTROL BUSINESS CYCLES

The business cycles are generally considered as the hurdles to the smooth and orderly progress of economy or society. So, naturally, business cycles must be controlled to attain economic stability. Economists advocate different measures to control business cycles as under:

(i) Monetary Measures: Prof. Hawtrey, Prof. Hayek and some other economists argued that trade cycle is a monetary phenomenon. So it can be controlled by formulating suitable monetary policy. Monetary policy is the government policy formulated to control the supply of money including bank credit in circulation in the economy. There are three types of monetary policies, viz. (i) dear or tight money policy, (ii) cheap money policy, and (iii) neutral money policy.

Monetary policy consists of monetary measures like bank rate policy, open market operation, cash reserve ratio and qualitative credit control measures. These are also known as central bank credit control measures—quantitative and qualitative measures.

The tight money policy is being used to control inflation or boom. It is called anti-inflationary measure. Under tight money policy, the bank rate will be raised; government bonds and securities will be sold by tender and taping methods; cash reserve ratio will be raised; the margin of requirement on loans against securities will be raised; the purposes and maximum limit of loans will be controlled and other directions will be issued by the central bank of the country. These measures make bank loans costlier so it reduces supply of bank credit on one hand and on the other they reduce the supply of money in circulation in the economy. Thus, it controls boom or inflation.

The cheap money policy is being used to control depression or deflation. It is called anti-deflationary measure. Under cheap money policy, the bank rate will be reduced; government bonds and securities will be purchased back from the public; cash reserve ratio will be reduced; the margin of requirement on loans against securities will be reduced; the purposes and maximum limit of loans will be relaxed and other directions will be issued by the central bank of the country. These measures make bank loans cheaper so it increases supply of bank credit on one hand and on the other they raise the supply of money in circulation in the economy. Thus, it controls depression or deflation.

(ii) Fiscal Measures: The monetary policy alone may not sufficient to check business fluctuations. Therefore, it is suggested that monetary policy should be properly integrated with a suitable fiscal policy to achieve the desired results. Keynes and his followers such as Alvin Hansen and others, have recommended compensatory finance or compensatory fiscal policy to bring about stabilization of business activity. It is, therefore, suggested that the government should regulate its activities in such a manner as to offset the cyclical fluctuations in private business activity.

The fiscal policy is the government policy formulated to achieve the objectives like full employment, economic growth and stability, etc. The fiscal policy consists of three main instruments, viz. (a) taxation, (b) public expenditure, and (c) public borrowing.

To fight boom or inflation, under fiscal policy, (i) the government imposes new taxes and raises existing tax rates on income, commodities and services to control the excess demand, (ii) the government reduces unproductive and non-essential public expenditures to reduce the supply of money-income, and (iii) the government sells its bonds and securities to public and borrow more loans from public which reduces purchasing power of the people.

To fight depression or deflation, under fiscal policy, (i) the government removes some taxes and reduces existing tax rates on income, commodities and services to encourage the demand, (ii) the government raises unproductive and non-essential public expenditures to increase the supply of money-income, and (iii) the government buys back its bonds and securities from public and repays the loans borrowed from public which increases purchasing power of the people.

It is in-built mechanism that works automatically to avoid the occurrence of boom and depression in the economy. It is being regulated through surplus or deficit budget policy. Surplus budget policy will be used to control boom and deficit budget policy will be used to control the depression.

(iii) Public Works Policy: During depression, economic activity is low at low ebb, and consequently there is considerable unemployment, the propensity to consume is naturally low. The government should undertake the autonomous investment for public works activities to fight the depression. The public works expenditure of the government will have thus performed the function of 'priming the pump' of economic activity in the country.

But there is another function that government spending programme may be made to perform, namely that of stabilizing economic activity over a long period and making it free from booms and depressions by constantly and appropriately adjusting public investment to the changes in the private investment.

(iv) State Control of Investment: According to Keynes, the business expectation governed investments vary more and create more ups and downs in the free capitalist economy so socialization of investment is necessary to control the business cycles.

(v) Direct Controls: Sometimes, direct government controls over prices and wages as a measure against inflation or deflation are advocated to control the trade cycle. It is essential to make monetary and fiscal measures more effective. Imposing ceiling on price, wage-rate, profit-rate, production of selected goods, etc. direct control measure will help to control boom and their relaxations would control depression.

(vi) Socialistic Measures: Socialistic economists like Karl Marx thought that the business cycle is the outcome of the capitalistic society. In a capitalistic economy, the profit motive being the main objective of investment fluctuations in business activity are bound to occur. There will not be wide fluctuations in the business activity in the socialistic economy as the investment is planned and controlled by the Central Planning Authority. The best way to avoid business cycles is to adopt socialism. If one has to accept this advice, he has to make a choice between the two evils.

(vii) International Measures: In case of open-economy, trade cycle is an international phenomenon. Any form of economic instability spread from country to country in trade contact. The important measures suggested to trade cycles at international level are: (a) international production control, (b) international buffer stock-operations and (c) international investment production control.

In brief, monetary, fiscal and direct control measures would prevent the occurrence of trade cycles if they are devised at right time.

5.4 MODEL QUESTIONS

2-Marks Questions

1. What is trade cycle?
2. Give definition on business cycle.
3. Name any two features of trade cycle.
4. Name the phases of trade cycle.
5. What is economic depression?
6. What is economic recession?
7. What is economic revival?
8. What is economic boom?
9. What is full employment?
10. Name any two causes of trade cycle.
11. Give the central idea of Hawtrey's trade cycle theory.
12. Give the central idea of Keynes' trade cycle theory.
13. Give the central idea of Schumpeter's trade cycle theory.
14. Suggest any two trade cycle control measures.

5-Marks Questions

1. Write a brief note on features of trade cycle.
2. Discuss briefly the phases of trade cycle.
3. Write a short note on Hawtrey's trade cycle theory.
4. Write a short note on Keynes' trade cycle theory.
5. Write a short note on Schumpeter's trade cycle theory.
6. Discuss briefly the trade cycle control measures.

10-Marks Questions

1. Define trade cycle. Explain its features.
2. Define trade cycle. Explain its phases.
3. Critically examine Hawtrey's pure monetary theory.
4. Discuss Keynes' trade cycle theory.
5. Explain critically Schumpeter's trade cycle theory.
6. Discuss the measures to control trade cycles.

Glossary

Consumption Function: This concept is first introduced by J.M. Keynes. It relates the level of consumption expenditure to the level of income.

Average Propensity to Consume (APC): It indicates the ratio of aggregate consumption expenditure to aggregate income, i.e. it is the ratio of C to Y and is expressed as C/Y.

Average Propensity to Save (APS): The relation between aggregate incomes to aggregate savings, i.e. S/Y.

External Forces: Forces other than demand and supply. For example, government, central bank and any other external factors.

Classicals: Classical economists.

Free Market Price System: It is also known as 'Price Mechanism' or 'Market Mechanism'.

Depression: A phase of trade cycle where all economic activities are at bottom or slump.

Great Depression: A depression which occurred in Wall Street, New York of USA and later spread all over the world during 1930s.

Economy: Economic system of country.

Community: People of a country or economy.

Marginal Productivity of Labour: Productivity of additional unit of labour.

Producing Capacity: Capacity of producing goods and services.

Labour Force: Supply of working age group population.

Time-elements: Time factor, the time factor is general divided in two types of duration, namely (i) short-run and (ii) long-run.

Consumer Goods: The goods which directly satisfy the consumers' wants.

Capital Goods: Machines, tools, buildings, etc. which are used to produce consumers' goods.

Multiplier Effect: It is known as investment or income multiplier effect. The extent of income generated due to increment of investment through the value of marginal property to consume.

Investment: Employment of fund on capital goods like machines, buildings, etc. or net addition to capital stock or purchase of new machines, buildings, etc.

Rate of Interest: Price paid to the service of capital. Or price paid to capital or money for parting with liquidity.

Planned Savings: Deliberately saving for some purposes. It is also known as 'intended savings' or ex-ante savings.

Planned Investment: Deliberately undertaking of investment. It is also known as 'Intended Investment' or 'Ex-ante Investment'.

Objective Factors: Keynes suggested six objective factors which influence on consumption function. These are: fiscal policy, corporate financial policy changes in expectations, windfall gains or losses, liquidity assets and rate of interest.

Subjective Factors: Keynes suggested eight subjective factors which influence on consumption function. These are: precaution, prudent, calculation, improvement of standard of living, independence, enterprise pride and avarice.

Acceleration: Important tool of economic analysis. It shows effect of a change in consumption on investment. It is also known as 'Relation'.

Marginal Propensity to Save (MPS): It is opposite of marginal propensity to consume. It can be derived from MPC, the reason is that MPC plus MPS=1. Hence, MPS=1–MPC. The term first used by Keynes.

Real Investment: Real investment implies the creation of new capital goods such as machinery, factory buildings, plants, etc. These create additional jobs and new output.

Financial Investment: Financial investment means the purchase of existing paper securities, bonds, debentures or equities or second hand assets and these have no effect on the employment position.

Autonomous: Investment made independent of income is autonomous investment.

Induced Investment: Induced investment is that investment which arises on account of changes in income. It depends on interest rate and MEC.

Inflationary Gap: It refers to the excess of anticipated expenditure over availability of output at a full employment economy.

Supply Price of Capital Asset: Keynes' calls the cost of acquiring an asset as its supply price.

Prospective Yields: It refers profit expectations from the capital asset over its average life.

Demand Price of Capital Asset: Demand price of an asset is defined as the sum of the expected future yields discounted at the current rate of interest.

Investment Multiplier: Keynesian concept which establishes relationship between initial increase in investment and the final increase in aggregate income through changes in consumption-expenditures. It shows how much of additional income is being generated from change in autonomous investment. In terms of a formula it is written as $k=\Delta Y/\Delta I$ or $= 1/1-MPC$. It is read as k is equal to the reciprocal of 1–MPC, where k is multiplier and MPC is marginal propensity to consume.

Innovation: It means the introduction of something new, say the introduction of either new goods or services, or new techniques of producing them. Innovation is a vital factor in economic growth. The desire to increase profit is the main incentive for business innovations.

Bank Credit: The banks lend to their customers by granting loans or overdraft to them when banks increase their loans and advances they also increase their deposit. This type of a lending is known as Bank Credit.

Cheap Money: It is a situation in which credit is easily available at relatively low rate of interest.

Bank Rate Policy: As lender of the last resort, the central bank helps the commercial banks in temporary need of cash when other sources of raising cash are exhausted. And increase in the bank rate would discourage commercial banks to borrow from the central bank and a corresponding increase in the lending rate of commercial banks to general public would decrease public borrowing from banks.

Open Market Operations: The central bank can enter the money market for the purpose of purchaser sale of government securities on its own account.

Entrepreneur: A business owner or the manager who risks his own money and uses his own money and uses his own judgment and ability to make profit.

Effective Demand: According to Keynes, the level of income and employment in a capitalist economy depends upon what is calls "effective demand" comprising total expenditure on consumption and expenditure on investment. Changes in total expenditure therefore imply changes in effective demand which, in its turn, lead to changes in income and employment in the country.

Unique Apparatus: Without a like or equal set of implements.

Liquidity Preference: The desired of people to hold money is called the liquidity preference, Keynes maintains that people desired to hold money for three purposes. These are: Transactions purposes, precautionary purposes and speculative purposes.

Invention: Inventing; thing invented.

Propitious: Favourable; of good omen.

Endogenous Factors: These are integral to the economic structure and operate within the economic system. They include common variables such as the volume of bank credit, interest, interest rate, the price level, the elasticity of supply of production factors, etc. These factors are primarily responsible for the periodic wave-like movements.

Phenomenon Species: Apparent objects or facts, remarkable persons or things; a wonder.

Momentum: Quantity of motion of a moving body.

Replica: Duplicate of a picture or pieces of sculpture of the artist himself.

Amplitude: Maximum departure from average of an oscillation-alternating current spaciousness; abundance.

Cumulative: Increasing or increased progressively in amount, force, etc.

Capitalism: Economic and political system depend upon on private capital and profit-making.

Pessimism: Tendency to be gloomy or expect the worst.

Venture: Risky Undertaking commercial speculation—expose to risk stake.

Crisis: Time of danger or great difficulty in financial matter.

Recur: Occur again; be repeated.

Retrieve: Regain, possession of possibility of recovery.

Boom: A term used to describe a period of rapid expansion in business activities, resulting in high stock and commodity prices, high profit, and low unemployment. A boom does not last for a long period of time and is soon followed by a bust.

Bust: It refers to a drop in overall business activity to an extremely low level, resulting in low prices, low profits, low income, and high unemployment. Busts invariably follow booms.

REFERENCE BOOKS

Dudley Dillard (1960): The Economics of John Maynard Keynes London. Grosbylock D. & Sons Ltd.

Seth M.L. (1983): *An Introduction to Keynesian Economics,* Laxmi Narain Agarwal, Agra.

Gupta R.D. (1983): *Keynisian Economics*, Kalyani Publishers Rajinder Nagar, Ludhiana.

Dewett K.K. (1993): *Modern Economic Theory,* S. Chand & Company Ltd., New Delhi.

Ahuja H. .L (2002): *Macroeconomics Theory and Policy,* S. Chand & Company Ltd., New Delhi.

M.L. Seth: *Macroeconomics,* Lakshmi Narain Agarwal Publication, Agra.

JM. Keynes: *The General Theory of Employment Interest and Money.*

M.L. Jhingan: *Advanced Economic Theory,* 8th Edition, Konark Publications, Haryana.

K.K. Dewett: *Modern Economic Theory*, 21st edition, Shyamlal Charitable Trust, New Delhi.

H.L. Ahuja: *Modern Economics,* 6th Editions. S. Chand & Co Ltd, New Delhi.

K.P.M. Sundram and M C Vaish: *Principles of Economics*, Ratan Prakhashan Educational Publishers.

Jhingon M.L.: *Macroeconomics Theory,* Konark Publishers Private Ltd., Delhi.

A.H. Hansen: *A Guide to Keynes,* Delhi.

K.P.M. Sundharam: *Money. Banking and International Trade,* Sultan Chand and Sons, Educational Pblishers 23, Daryaganj, New Delhi.

T.N. Hajela: *A Textbook of Monetary Economics*, Shiva Lal Agarwala and Company, Agra.